Ethical Business
Leadership

Studies in Theoretical and Applied Ethics

Sherwin Klein
General Editor

Vol. 7

PETER LANG
New York • Washington, D.C./Baltimore • Bern
Frankfurt am Main • Berlin • Brussels • Vienna • Oxford

Sherwin Klein

Ethical Business Leadership

Balancing Theory and Practice

PETER LANG
New York • Washington, D.C./Baltimore • Bern
Frankfurt am Main • Berlin • Brussels • Vienna • Oxford

Library of Congress Cataloging-in-Publication Data

Klein, Sherwin.
Ethical business leadership: balancing theory and practice / Sherwin Klein.
p. cm. — (Studies in theoretical and applied ethics; vol. 7)
Includes bibliographical references and index.
1. Business ethics. 2. Social responsibility of business. 3. Leadership.
I. Title. II. Studies in theoretical and applied ethics; v. 7.
HF5387 .K577   658.4'08—dc21   2001038341
ISBN 0-8204-5710-8
ISSN 1086-6809

Die Deutsche Bibliothek-CIP-Einheitsaufnahme

Klein, Sherwin:
Ethical business leadership: balancing theory and practice / Sherwin Klein.
–New York; Washington, D.C./Baltimore; Bern;
Frankfurt am Main; Berlin; Brussels; Vienna; Oxford: Lang.
(Studies in theoretical and applied ethics; Vol. 7)
ISBN 0-8204-5710-8

The paper in this book meets the guidelines for permanence and durability
of the Committee on Production Guidelines for Book Longevity
of the Council of Library Resources.

© 2002 Peter Lang Publishing, Inc., New York

Printed in the United States of America

To my sons Chuck and Dave

Acknowledgments

I received aid and encouragement from anonymous reviewers of my published articles, which form the basis of this book; they helped me to avoid mistakes I otherwise would have made. I am grateful to Professor Robert J. Baum, Editor of *Business and Professional Ethics Journal*, who, since my first publication in his journal in 1990, has been supportive of my work. I wish to thank Phyllis Korper of Peter Lang Publishing for her help in publishing the book. I am most indebted to my wife, Eleanor, whose love, patience, and constant support of my work have been indispensable to me.

I also wish to thank the following editors for allowing me to use modified versions of my articles (listed below), which were published in their journals: Professor Robert J. Baum, Editor of *Business and Professional Ethics Journal*, Professor Elliot D. Cohen, Editor of the *International Journal of Applied Philosophy*, and Professor George G. Brenkert, Editor-in-Chief of the *Business Ethics Quarterly*.

The following is a list of articles I have written that have been used, in a more or less modified form, in this book and the chapters in which they appear. Chapter 1: "Drucker's Knowledge Society and Socratic *Sōphrosynē*," *Business and Professional Ethics Journal*, vol. 12, #4 (Winter 1993): 51–71. Chapter 2: "*Don Quixote* and the Problem of Idealism and Realism in Business Ethics," *Business Ethics Quarterly*, vol. 8, #1 (1998): 43–63. Reprinted by permission of the *Business Ethics Quarterly*. Chapter 3: "An Aristotelian View of Theory and Practice in Business Ethics," *International Journal of Applied Philosophy*, vol. 12, #2 (Fall 1998): 203–222. Reprinted by permission of the *International Journal of Applied Philosophy*. Chapter 4: "An Aristotelian Approach to

Ethical Corporate Leadership," *Business and Professional Ethics Journal*, vol. 14, #3 (Fall 1995): 3–23. Chapter 5: "Emotions and Practical Reasoning: Implications for Business Ethics," *Business and Professional Ethics Journal*, vol. 17, #3 (1998): 3–29. Reprinted by permission of *Business and Professional Ethics Journal*. In Chapter 5, I have also used portions of "The Head, The Heart, and Business Virtues," to be published in a forthcoming issue of the *Journal of Business Ethics*. Reprinted by permission of Kluwer Academic Publishers.

The costs associated with preparing the manuscript were defrayed by a grant from Fairleigh Dickinson University. I wish to thank the committee that awarded the grant to me.

Contents

Preface

This book is based upon articles in business ethics, which I wrote in the 1990s. These articles have been revised so that they now form chapters—rather than independent articles–which develop the related themes of ethical business leadership and theory and practice in business ethics.

As is the case with my first book in business ethics—*Business Ethics: Reflections from a Platonic Point of View*—this work takes, what may broadly be called, a virtue ethics position. Classical virtue ethics was developed by Plato and Aristotle. Aristotle is more popular than Plato among virtue ethics theorists who engage in contemporary discussions of business ethics. Possibly, this is due to the fact that recent interest in virtue ethics has been sparked by Aristotelians—or, at least, philosophers who recognize Aristotle's importance in the history of ethical theory. My first business ethics book was written, in part, to show that Plato is an important source of insight for business ethicists. Much of what I believe to be Plato's major contributions to contemporary business ethics are considered in this book. Although Plato still takes center stage in the first chapter of my present book, Aristotle's virtue ethics (and his practical philosophy in general) is more prominent in the last three chapters.

I have not limited myself to Plato's and Aristotle's contributions to business ethics. In the second chapter, *Don Quixote*, one of the great novels of the western world, is used to develop our themes, and in the final chapter, I turn to science as well as philosophy to support my contention that virtue ethics should play a central role in theorizing about ethical decision-making in business. Aristotle's theory of ethical decision-making is seen to fit well with contemporary scientific findings and thoughtful reflections on the relation between emotions and reasoning.

The first chapter considers Peter F. Drucker's version of a post-capitalist society—one in which specialized workers are employed in organizations with specialized missions. Since he is arguably the dean of management theorists, it is appropriate to consider his vision of such a society. However, his discussion of ethical organizational leadership in such a society is found wanting. I argue that the Platonic Socrates' conception of statesmanship, derived from an analysis of Plato's *Charmides*, is preferable to the suggestions concerning leadership that Drucker offers. Plato's notion of statesmanship, which is seen to be grounded in his view of dialectic and the liberal arts, is shown to provide beneficial guidance to Drucker's society of specialized workers employed in specialized organizations.[1]

Although in Chapter 1 I defend the Platonic Socrates' conception of statesmanship, many people consider the Platonic philosopher king (the model Platonic statesman) to be a quixotic concept (in a negative sense)—an idealistic fantasy with little or no practical value. Therefore, in Chapter 2, I discuss the novel *Don Quixote* in order to consider the place of idealistic theory and realistic practice in business ethics. I suggest that the mutual influence of Don Quixote and Sancho Panza may serve as a model for achieving a balance between idealistic theoreticians and common sense realists in business and business ethics. The novel stimulates our imaginations to conceive of the possibility of a fruitful dialogue between such people with radically different views. With reference to our concern for examining the nature of ethical business leadership, I maintain that one possible interpretation of Plato's philosopher king is what I call a quixotified Sancho Panza (Sancho educated by Don Quixote). This combination of the idealism and wisdom of Don Quixote and the realism and practicality of Sancho Panza is suggested as a model for managerial statesmanship—a model which provides a balance between the extremes of rootless theory (unsanchofied Don Quixote) and narrow practicality (unquixotified Sancho Panza). I discuss the possibility of business accepting such a leadership model. The concept of a quixotified Sancho Panza as ethical business leader is supported by contemporary discussions of leadership, and the ethical implications of one "quixotic" vision for business are considered.

Chapter 3 develops an Aristotelian view of theory and practice with respect to issues in business ethics. In the first part of the chapter, I show that Aristotle's political philosophy exhibits a proper balance between theory and practice, and his discussions are pertinent to considerations of corporate culture. Since ethical corporate leadership requires the creation and maintenance of moral corporate cultures, I suggest that Aristotle's discussion of "constitutions," which is close in meaning to "corporate cultures," would be helpful to business leaders. Aristotle's political philosophy is based upon his ethical philosophy—his theory of virtue. I argue that an Aristotelian business ethics would apply Aristotle's concept of virtue to corporations so that neither the experiential or practice-based features of corporate cultures nor the more theory-based ethical consider-ations are overemphasized. I contend that Aristotelian business ethics is neither as overly theory-laden as business ethics that relies heavily on modern ethical theory nor is it excessively experience- or practice-based. In the second part of the chapter, I argue that Aristotle's analysis of practical wisdom—a concept essential to ethical corporate leadership—ex-hibits a delicate balance between theory and practice. This balance is not evident in the heavily theory-laden positions of a number of business ethicists who rely on modern ethical theory and, therefore, on the application of moral rules and principles to problems in business ethics.

I agree with the position, accepted by many business ethicists, that a theory of managerial or corporate responsibility which considers the impact of management's decisions on stakeholders—e.g., customers, employees, suppliers, and the general public—as well as shareholders is ethically preferable to one which considers the impact of management's decisions on shareholders alone. The ethical corporate leader, in Platonic and Aristotelian fashion, should be able to recognize and implement what is good for the whole and distribute goods justly—balance, in a fair manner, the legitimate, though often competing, claims of stakeholders. However, in Chapter 4, after discussing the above position, I suggest that apart from the question of whether or not business will accept a stakeholder, rather than a shareholder, view of managerial responsibility, there remains the vexing problem of a just implementation of a stakehold-er view of managerial responsibility, i.e., a fair balancing of the interests of legitimate constituents. In this chapter, I use Aristotle to help to both localize and solve the central problem with respect to determining a just distribution of corporate goods. We see Aristotle, as the *phronimos* or practically wise person, in action solving what may well be the most difficult ethical problem for corporate leaders.

In Chapter 5, I use the scientific findings and conclusions of Antonio R. Damasio and the philosophical reflections of Ronald de Sousa to support the position, argued for in Chapter 3, that Aristotelian virtue ethics provides a better account of ethical decision-making—and therefore ethical practice—than does modern ethical theory. Damasio and de Sousa show that emotions and feelings are indispensable to the proper functioning of practical reasoning. A character- or virtue-based ethics, such as Aristotle's, which emphasizes the proper nurturing of emotions or passions, is seen to be necessary for practical (and therefore business) ethics, for it is necessary for proper ethical decision-making. In the epilogue to the chapter, I argue that support from requisite feelings or emotions is necessary for the possibility of objective rationality, and I use Robert H. Frank's examples to show that emotions can help to resolve certain ethical dilemmas—and therefore certain ethical business dilemmas.

Notes

1. I shall use the terms "statesman" and "statesmanship" to imply ethical leadership. Moreover, the term "ethical leadership," as I use it, implies practical wisdom. I agree with contemporary writers on leadership who suggest that true business leaders are capable of understanding ideals and presenting them as visions, which encapsulate the values they espouse. They also have the ability to deal with the details that put their visions into practice. The values of ethical leadership—"leadership" in its honorific sense is ethical—are expressed in visions that benefit all persons affected by the implementation of the visions.

CHAPTER I

Drucker's Knowledge Society and Socratic *Sōphrosynē*

Introduction

In the first section, I consider Peter F. Drucker's version of a post-capitalist society, in which management applies knowledge to knowledge itself so that, as he says, "existing knowledge can best be applied to produce results" (PCS, 42).[1] Post-capitalist society is described as a society of organizations consisting of two tiers of specialized functions—those of organizations and of workers within these organizations. He believes that the specialized functions of organizations determine the limits of their social responsibility. I argue that Drucker's position on the social responsibility of organizations is inadequate. He does suggest that someone like the traditional educated person is still needed to provide guidance in this post-capitalist society, but he provides no clear picture of who he or she is; nor does he show clearly what sort of knowledge is required of this person. Thus, we are still left with a question which is central to business ethics, what is effective, ethical business leadership?

In the second section, using Plato's discussion of *sōphrosynē* in the *Charmides*, I attempt to shed some light on the issue of ethical business leadership. Drucker denies that there is a "queen of the knowledges," but the Platonic Socrates shows that the philosopher as dialectician can provide beneficial guidance to a society of organizations in Drucker's post-capitalist society by supplying a method for determining the truth (or, at least, searching for it) and by providing some aid in discovering knowledge of the good.

The Socratic/Platonic conception of the liberal arts is based upon the above two features of the dialectician—characteristics which are implied by the Socratic/Platonic conception of self-knowledge. In the third section, I elaborate upon this view of the liberal arts and contrast it with the Protagorean version. This is necessary in order adequately to understand why the Socratic/Platonic conception of the liberal arts succeeds in providing some proper guidance to Drucker's society of specialized organizations, while Drucker fails to provide such guidance.

A Critique of Drucker's Notion of Leadership in a Post-Capitalist Society

In the first part of Drucker's book, *Post-Capitalist Society*, he traces the transformation of what he calls the meaning of knowledge—actually its referent—from being to doing; from something private "it became a resource and a utility" (PCS, 19). He maintains that Plato's and Protagoras's theories dominated the West's beliefs concerning knowledge. Plato, through Socrates, advocated self-knowledge as the purpose of knowledge while Protagoras emphasized logic, grammar, and rhetoric—which constituted the core of the liberal arts. In both cases, Drucker suggests that knowledge was distinguished from *technē* or skill, that is, the ability to know from the ability to do. He argues that although Socrates and Protagoras both respected *technē*, it was not considered knowledge because "it was confined to one specific application and had no general principles" (PCS, 27). Second, a *technē* is learned through experience and Drucker seems to think that a *technē* is not knowledge because having no general principles, it could not be taught as knowledge.[2]

The first step in knowledge becoming "a resource and a utility" was its application in developing "tools, processes, products"—*technē* becomes technology; that is, craft knowledge as "organized, systematic, purposeful knowledge" (PCS, 28) was developed and taught, e.g., as engineering, agriculture, mining, and medicine (from about the middle of the 18th century). The second step—from 1880 to the end of World War II—involved an application of knowledge to work; this ushered in a "productivity revolution." According to Drucker, F. W. Taylor was the seminal thinker in determining how manual work could be made productive.[3] The third and last phase he discusses began after World War II and will continue into the unforeseeable future. This revolutionary phase—the management revolution—is attributed to management, and its essence is the application of knowledge to knowledge itself. This chapter is concerned with this phase in the application of knowledge. With this third application of knowledge, we are thrust into a post-capitalist society.

> Supplying knowledge to find out how existing knowledge can best be applied to produce results is, in effect, what we mean by management. But knowledge is now being applied systematically and purposefully to define what *new* knowledge is needed, whether it is feasible, and what has to be done to make knowledge effective. It is being applied, in other words, to systematic innovation (PCS, 42).

Drucker reminds us that he is uniquely qualified to write about this phase. His "'The Practice of Management' ... first established management as a discipline in 1954" (PCS, 43). However, business management is only one example of management; management is "a generic function of all organizations" (PCS, 43). Like the three phases in the application of knowledge, the meaning of "management," according to Drucker, has undergone three changes since World War II. Originally, a manager was defined as "someone who is responsible for the work of subordinates"—a boss—but by the early 1950s, its meaning changed to one who "is responsible for the performance of people." Today, it means one who "is responsible for the application and performance of knowledge" (PCS, 44). Knowledge is management's essential resource and its management is the definition of this profession.

As a modern resource, knowledge is highly specialized; it is "knowledges." The knowledge of the traditionally educated—Socratic knowledge of the self and Protagorean knowledge of rhetoric or "image"—"are not tools for deciding *what to do* and how to do it" (PCS, 46).

> The knowledge we now consider knowledge proves itself in action. What we now mean by knowledge is information effective in action, information fo-

cused on results. These results are seen *outside* the person—in society and economy, or in the advancement of knowledge itself (PCS, 46).

This knowledge requires specialists rather than the generalists. Drucker recognizes that this emphasis in society on specialized knowledges raises questions of values, vision, and the nature of the educated person in society (PCS, 47). I should think that one also would have to say that it raises the question, what is management? Moreover, Drucker is presenting a challenge to people like myself who believe that Socratic self-knowledge and the liberal arts are essential to management in Drucker's (modern) sense.

Drucker develops the importance of the specialist's knowledge in the following way. Although specialization in knowledge greatly increases the performance potential in the different areas of these knowledges, these specialized knowledges must be connected to turn potential into performance (PCS, 192–193). Therefore, the emphasis on knowledges necessitates organization. Drucker says that "The function of organizations is to make knowledge productive" (PCS, 49). They do this by coordinating specialists' knowledges—giving them unified forms. But organizations, themselves, are defined in terms of specialized functions—"organizations are special purpose institutions" (PCS, 53). The goals of specialists are subject specific and must be integrated under the umbrella values of organizations, which are mission specific.

Drucker is concerned with the social responsibility of organizations. He tells us that an organization should stick to its peculiar function; that is, an organization should recognize that having a specialized function, its function determines the limits of its competence. Thus, he argues that businesspeople invariably fail when they seek political power, for they are not exercising their "proper function." He argues, I think correctly, that "organizations can only do damage to themselves and to society if they tackle tasks that are beyond their specialized competence, their specialized functions" (PCS, 101). However, he asks, who else can care for society when "these organizations collectively *are* society" (PCS, 101)? "Organizations do have a responsibility to find an approach to basic social problems that can match their competence and can, in fact, render social problems an opportunity for the organization" (PCS, 102).

Drucker also thinks that organizations must myopically believe that their specialized task is "the most important task in society" in order to perform well. Somehow, "collectively, they discharge the tasks of society" (PCS, 99–100). When organizations conflict, there are "no hard and fast answers" for resolving the conflicts, except that the survival of society overrides the survival of any of its "organs" (PCS, 100).

It seems to me that Drucker's analysis of the social responsibility of organizations unravels because it is tied to the competence of specialists and to specialized functions rather than, to use his term, the competencies and functions of "generalists." However, Drucker does suggest that someone like the traditional educated person (the traditional humanist's ideal of the "universally educated person") is still needed because "the knowledge society is a society of knowledges and … it is global—in its money, its economics, its careers, its technology, its central issues, and above all, in its information" (PCS, 211). In this society, there must, then, be a unifying force. "It requires a leadership group, which can focus local, particular, separate traditions onto a common and shared commitment to values, a common concept of excellence, and on mutual respect" (PCS, 212). He argues that the humanists are correct in emphasizing the importance of "a universally educated person," but a bridge to the classics is not enough, for humanistic education does not show how this knowledge applies to the present and the future. He suggests that humanists show no concern for *this*. Drucker argues that liberal arts education was meaningful for his generation, but today students often fail to see the relevance of this education. "Their liberal education … does not enable them to understand reality, let alone master it" (PCS, 213). Thus, while Drucker leaves an opening for the generalist in a post-capitalist society, and even professes to be sympathetic to the value of traditional humanistic education, his generalist does not seem to be an educated person in either, as he would put it, a Socratic or a Protagorean sense, i.e., one who is devoted to either Socratic self-knowledge or to humanistic learning (learning associated with the liberal arts).

We have seen, however, that Drucker suggests that in a post-capitalist society, the educated person (who resembles the humanist's ideal of the "universally educated person") is needed. How can Drucker's generalist resemble such an ideal when he or she is neither a Socratic nor a Protagorean (in Drucker's sense)? Not only does Drucker fail to answer this question, he does not show clearly what the knowledge of his educated person is and how it applies to the present and the future. In the final chapter—"The Educated Person"—it is difficult to see the application of the ideal of "a universally educated person" to organizational life as he sees it, and the reason is not far to seek. We have seen that, according to Drucker, post-capitalist society as a knowledge society needs specialists and as a society of organizations requires managers. Managers do not place the value on *technai* that specialists do, for *technai* are seen as means to organizational goals. These goals, themselves, are specialized; they are the goals of organizations with specialized missions. The two cultures, then, are guided by specialists of different sorts. Drucker argues that it would be advisable for members of each culture to experience one another's cultures. However, such broadening experience is not liberal in the traditional sense. He argues that the liberal arts curriculum is a failure because it stubbornly refuses to integrate these knowledges—as a "universe of knowledge"—into its curriculum. But not to do so, according to Drucker, is not liberal, for it fails to create "a universe of discourse"—mutual understanding. The very advance of knowledge requires an understanding of the connecting links among these knowledges as he suggests a number of times. However, he believes that there is no "queen of the knowledges" in the knowledge society—no counterpart to philosophy. Who, then, can properly provide the regulative knowledge that can guide a society of organizations in Drucker's post-capitalist era, and what kind(s) of knowledge is necessary? In the next section, I shall argue that in the *Charmides*, Plato provides reasonable answers to these questions. In analyzing *sōphrosynē*, he examines the question of whether or not philosophy, as Drucker puts it, is the "queen of the knowledges"? We shall see that, in the *Charmides*, the Platonic Socrates uncovers difficulties with this notion, as does Drucker, but he provides suggestions that, when developed, help one to understand how philosophy, as the "queen" of the liberal arts, can shed light on the above questions about which Drucker leaves us in the dark—who can provide the knowledge necessary for guiding society as a society of organizations, and what kind(s) of knowledge is necessary to guide such a society properly?

Drucker's Post-Capitalist Society and Platonic *Sōphrosynē*

The subject of the *Charmides*, *sōphrosynē*, cannot be translated in any straightforward way into English, although most often it is translated as temperance. To the ancient Greek, it denoted the highest ideal. *Sōphrosynē* is the foundation of the two famous sayings associated with the Delphic Oracle—"nothing in excess" and "know thyself." The former notion connotes moderation and therefore self-control—control of sexual passion and the desire for wealth, power, and ambition. In a broader sense, *sōphrosynē* connotes not going beyond due limits, keeping due measure, having a sense of proportion and a harmonious soul. It is no wonder, then, that it also carries the meaning, health or soundness of mind and wisdom in the broadest sense (including discretion and sound judgment). It is not possible to have this virtue in the fullest sense without also following the Delphic maxim, "know thyself." According to Socrates, to know oneself includes knowing that the soul (*psuchē*) not the body ought to be the ruling element; therefore, to know oneself is to be self-controlled. Self-knowledge, according to Plato, implies knowledge of human capabilities and, specifically, of one's own abilities and is essential to the philosopher king of the *Republic*, for on this principle, he or she orders the ideal city. To go beyond the limitations of human nature and specifically of one's own nature is *hubris*. Socratic *sōphrosynē* manifests this humility in the highest sense. As Plato says in the *Apology*, the oracle at Delphi says that no person is wiser than Socrates, and this is so, according to Socrates, because he recognizes his own ignorance and has the ability to show those who profess to be wise that they too are ignorant although they think they have knowledge.

I shall begin the discussion of *sōphrosynē* in the *Charmides* at the point in the dialogue at which the principal interlocutor, Critias, suggests that *sōphrosynē* is self-knowledge and professes agreement with the inscription "know thyself" at Delphi. For Socrates, being virtuous in the highest sense entails knowing that one's actions are good and this is linked to self-knowledge.

Socrates pursues the inquiry into self-knowledge by first questioning its practical value. *Technai* such as medicine and architecture produce practical results, but what practical results does self-knowledge produce?

Moreover, all *technai* have goals other than themselves as the objects of their knowledge. How, then, can *sōphrosynē* as self-knowledge be possible—be a type of knowledge? Thus, Socrates criticizes the view of *sōphrosynē* attributed to him, and we are reminded of Drucker's criticism of Socratic self-knowledge as not providing the tools "for deciding what to do and how to do it." Critias could have said that just as the work of the architect is something external, e.g., a building, and the work of the physician is something physical, i.e., health, so the work of *sōphrosynē* is mental or spiritual—the health of the soul (suggested at *Charm.* 156a and 157a–b). What is more practical or beneficial than psychic health? Since, according to Socrates, the *psuchē* is the true self, the highest human function is the care of the human soul. One might also suspect that the ability to know that one knows what one knows and does not know, as the ideal of Socratic dialectic, and Socratic self-knowledge are intimately related to one another and to the health of the soul—they are the foundation of psychic health.[4] Thus, when Critias refuses to admit that *sōphrosynē* is a science (knowledge) like other types of knowledge but is, rather, *the* "knowledge of other knowledges and of itself" (*Charm.* 166c), this transition from a definition of *sōphrosynē* as self-knowledge to a definition of this concept as knowledge of other knowledges and of itself seems abrupt and incoherent but is not. This new definition of *sōphrosynē* which is related to the view of philosophy as the "queen of the knowledges" (to use Drucker's expression) is clearly relevant to the problem of determining knowledge that can guide Drucker's two cultures—two levels of specialists. We saw, however, that Drucker denies that there is a "queen of the knowledges," and we shall now see that Socrates himself subjects this view to criticism.

Socrates suggests that since, according to Critias, *sōphrosynē* is a knowledge of itself and other knowledges, it must also be a knowledge of the absence of knowledge (ignorance). So this virtue enables one to determine what he and others know and do not know. Clearly, this should remind the reader of Socrates, but Socrates, himself, is critical of this view. How is it possible for there to be a science of itself and other sciences, and even if this were possible, of what use would it be? Thus, Socrates raises the same issues he mentioned in considering the definition of *sōphrosynē* as self-knowledge.

Consider the former point. All other mental activities have some object other than themselves, e.g., seeing, hearing, desiring; how, then, can there be a knowledge of itself (knowledge having itself as its object)? Consider the latter point. Let us assume that there is a science which can distinguish between knowing and not knowing x; of what practical use would this be to the *technai*? It would not bring knowledge of health to the physician or knowledge of justice to the statesman, and so on with the other *technai*. It will, then, have no practical value in determining *what* a practitioner of a *technē* must know, only that he knows something or does not know something. This science, it would seem, does not teach the practitioner of a *technē* to know what he knows, for knowledge is gained in each *technē* by means of some specific act, e.g., as knowledge of health is gained; it is not gotten through *sōphrosynē*, in this example, but rather by the art of medicine. *Sōphrosynē* thus defined will not enable us to distinguish a pretender in any *technē* from an authentic practitioner. Of what value is it? It would seem that *technai* can be distinguished by their proper subject matter, and the practitioner of a *technē* must gain knowledge of the pertinent subject matter, not some knowledge of knowledge which appears to be irrelevant (of no practical use). Socrates suggests that he and Critias have searched in vain for this super science or *technē* which can guide society as a well-ordered whole (and we may include society as a complex of specialized organizations) by always being able to distinguish truth from error.

Socrates does uncover our qualms about a super science in the above sense, albeit in a technical way. If *sōphrosynē* in the above sense is not practical or even possible, the Socratic conception of dialectic (as a way of seeking knowledge) should be subject to the criticism of impracticality. We have seen that Drucker suggests that the present generation questions the practical value of the liberal arts. It "does not enable them to understand reality, let alone master it." At this point in the dialogue, Socrates is raising an analogous problem with dialectic. Nonetheless, we shall see that Socrates does show the practical value of dialectic as a way of determining that one knows what one knows and does not know (and in facilitating learning itself), and he also suggests the practical value of a super science—in the sense of one that attempts to gain knowledge of good and bad.

We are often reminded of the historical Socrates in the discussion of self-knowledge and the science of knowing that one knows what one knows and does not know. When Critias relates the inscription at Delphi—know thyself—to his definition of temperance as self-knowledge, the reader is reminded (at *Charm.* 164d–165b) of the Delphic Oracle's pronouncement that no man is wiser than Socrates and Socrates' interpretation (*Apology* 21a–23b). Socrates knows his own ignorance, but his interlocutors, e.g., those who possess specialized knowledge ("technicians"), claim knowledge beyond their specialties (see *Apology* 22d). Their dogmatism is deflated by Socrates' questions, for all inquiry-based learning begins in recognizing one's own ignorance.

Furthermore, *Charm.* 164d–165b is connected to section 167a, which is apparently modeled after Plato's picture of Socrates in the *Apology*.

> Then the wise or temperate man, and he only, will know himself, and be able to examine what he knows or does not know, and to see what others know and think that they know and do really know, and what they do not know and fancy that they know when they do not. No other person will be able to do this. And this is wisdom and temperance and self-knowledge—for a man to know what he knows, and what he does not know (*Charm.* 167a).

Socrates is evidently capable of knowing (recognizing) true and false craftsmen. But according to the formal argument of the *Charmides*, he should not be able to do this; it would seem that only a craftsman in craft x can evaluate another craftsman in craft x—i.e., distinguishing a true from a false craftsman demands knowledge specific to a craft. Suppose a person professes to be a good physician, but Socrates suspects that he is not. How can Socrates justify his suspicions if he is not a specialist in this *technē*? Euthyphro professes to know the nature of piety, but Socrates reveals that he is an imposter, not because of superior specialized knowledge, but because he exposes the inconsistencies in Euthyphro's beliefs. Socrates' knowledge of knowledge and ignorance, therefore, is based upon his ability to reason clearly and consistently. Socrates' method not only lays the foundation for problem solving, considered so essential to business thinking, but he knows how to ask the right questions and, from this, he determines what the problems are. As Drucker suggests, we hear a great deal about the importance of problem solving but not enough about the importance of localizing problems. The latter is the foundation of the former.

A knowledge of knowledge and ignorance is related to knowing that one knows what one knows and does not know in the following way. If we have a knowledge of knowledge, in one sense, we know when we know something as opposed to having a mere opinion or belief; we can recognize our knowledge. Therefore, we know *that* one knows what one knows and does not know. According to Socrates, Socratic dialectic provides the possibility of justifying one's opinions and, therefore, knowing *that* one knows what one knows and does not know. We see that Socratic self-knowledge is grounded in Socratic humility and Socratic humility when disciplined by Socratic dialectic, according to Plato, leads to justified opinions. I have argued elsewhere[5] that Socratic dialectic uses the opinions expressed by interlocutors—these are most often substantive *endoxa* (received opinions)—and these opinions are refuted by Socratic regulative *endoxa* (premises which are universally or widely accepted on reflection and are capable of guiding inquiry, e.g., virtue is a good and therefore is beneficial). The goal of such inquiry is justified opinion.

Although in this dialogue Socrates seems to be questioning his own position, and, as in other Socratic dialogues, we are left with no solution, he does suggest something positive about his dialectically derived wisdom. *Sōphrosynē*, as a knowledge of knowledge and ignorance,

> has this advantage—that he who possesses such knowledge will more easily learn anything which he learns, and that everything will be clearer to him, because, in addition to the several objects of knowledge, he sees the science, and this also will better enable him to test the knowledge which others have of what he knows himself, whereas the inquirer who is without this knowledge may be supposed to have a feebler and less effective insight.... Are not these, my friend, the real advantages which are to be gained from wisdom? And are not we looking and seeking after something more than is to be found in her (*Charm.* 172b–c)?

Here, Socrates connects dialectic with specialized knowledge and argues that dialectic makes learning easier and will make it easier to test another person's professed knowledge in his or her own specialty or specialties. Socratic dialectic is not only important in helping one to know that one knows what one knows and does not know, it is also important in learning how to acquire knowledge. Learning, as Drucker and others say, is learning how to learn, and Socrates has shown how the philosopher as dialectician can provide aid in the form of critical guidance to Drucker's society of organizations in his post-capitalist society.

But Socrates argues that *sōphrosynē* as a knowledge of what we know and do not know, even if we agree that such a science can distinguish truth from error, will not be sufficient for the creation of a good or happy society.

> Let us suppose that wisdom is such as we are now defining, and that she has absolute sway over us. Then, each action will be done according to the arts or sciences, and no one professing to be a pilot when he is not, no physician or general or anyone else pretending to know matters of which he is ignorant, will deceive or elude us. Our health will be improved; our safety at sea, and also in battle, will be assured; our coats and shoes, and all other instruments and implements will be skillfully made, because the workmen will be good and true.... Now I quite agree that mankind, thus provided, would live and act according to knowledge, for wisdom would watch and prevent ignorance from intruding on us in our work. But whether by acting according to knowledge we shall act well and be happy, my dear Critias—this is a point we have not yet been able to determine (*Charm.* 173a–d).

And Socrates maintains that a society of such perfect technicians is not necessarily a happy society. "It is not the life according to knowledge which makes men act rightly and be happy, not even if it be knowledge of all the sciences, but one science only, that of good and evil" (*Charm* 174 b–c). Technology, by itself, does not determine its own worth; only a knowledge of human benefit can do that.[6]

We have seen that Socratic self-knowledge is intimately related to Socratic humility, and self-knowledge is perfected by Socratic dialectic as a positive force for gaining knowledge. Socrates never practices dialectic for its own sake alone or for the sake of learning alone; it always has an ethical purpose. Therefore, the goal of the dialectician is knowledge of the good. It is in this sense, then, that the ruler, according to Plato, should be a philosopher and dialectic is a super science to be placed above all the other *technai* and sciences. In Socrates' society of technicians (*Charm.* 173a–d quoted above), each craftsman is knowledgeable in his or her own field; none, however, as a craftsman, has knowledge of the use of these types of knowledge for what is good or beneficial. How then, as Socrates suggests, can this society be happy? By accident? (See *Charm*. 174d.) Knowledge of what is good ought to guide such a society; that is, it ought to be governed by a philosopher king. In a society guided by the wise, all the crafts and the sciences would be directed to what is good—to the maximization of happiness in the society. Plato elaborates upon this position in the *Republic* where the statesman's wisdom guarantees justice by guiding the crafts. Justice, defined as doing one's own business, entails determining people's abilities and allowing for their development within the context of a whole. Socrates suggests that justice in this sense maximizes the city's happiness (however, not without compromises). Wisdom, therefore, requires self-knowledge in the sense of knowledge of the human soul—it requires *sōphrosynē*. Without this, no person or society can be happy; that is, without a knowledge of the human soul, there is no knowledge of the human good.[7]

Socratic self-knowledge, then, requires the two positive features of Socrates' idea of a "queen of the knowledges"—the practice of dialectic as a way of determining, or at least searching for, the truth and the goal of dialectic, knowledge of the good. The self-knowledge of the Socratic/Platonic dialectician, implying the above two notions, is the basis of the Socratic/Platonic conception of the liberal arts and helps to provide the knowledge that is capable of guiding Drucker's society of organizations. We can also determine who has such knowledge. The Socratic/Platonic view of the liberal arts requires elaboration and should be contrasted with the Protagorean position in order adequately to understand the force of the Socratic/Platonic view. To this end, we turn to the next and concluding section of the chapter.

Socratic/Platonic Vs. Protagorean Liberal Arts

In the first paragraph of Section 1, we saw that Drucker maintains that the subjects Protagoras emphasizes are the source of the liberal arts. Protagoras was perhaps the oldest and evidently the most famous of the professional sophists; he trained others for this profession and for other professions useful in public life. Little is known about Protagoras's works except through the possibly jaundiced eyes of Plato. His teaching emphasizes rhetoric, defined by Plato as the art of persuasion, and teaching students both sides of a case—the art of *logoi*. But the art of *logoi* does not purport to lead to the truth—and, therefore, differs from Socratic dialectic—because there is no such thing as falsehood, according to Protagoras, and therefore no such thing as truth. Protagoras says that man is the measure of all things and, therefore, what appears to him is true to him. He believes that the laws and customs that a city holds to be right are right as long as they are believed to be so. Socratic dialectic differs from Protagoras's art of *logoi* as a method which searches for the truth differs from one which attempts to persuade others to agree with one's position.[8] Plato criticizes Protagoras's art of *logoi* as being morally neutral—pertaining to means and not ends; we have seen that dialectic should be guided by a knowledge of good and bad. If opinion is king, as Protagoras thought, then the (sophistic) rhetorician, not the dialectician, can control people's minds, for knowledge, by definition, is stable but opinions are changeable—through persuasion.

It would seem that insofar as sophistic education is the core of the liberal arts, it provides a *technē* which is morally neutral alongside other morally neutral *technai* (of specialists). Sophistic humanism—of "a universally educated person"—can provide no more moral, or generally value, guidance than any other *technē* because truth, and therefore truth about values, is considered relative; value knowledge is reduced to opinion. Drucker's view that there is no "queen of the knowledges" (no philosopher king) is consistent with the above position, but then Drucker has no right to complain that practitioners of the liberal arts stubbornly refuse to integrate the knowledge of specialists into their curricula. On the basis of what knowledge can they do this? Contrary to Drucker, sophistic liberal arts education should help one to "master reality," while understanding or knowing it is not an issue since Protagoras's relativism reduces such knowledge to opinion. Indeed, businesspeople emphasize the importance of communication skills and rhetorical skills generally that one can learn from the liberal arts as particularly helpful to business. Certainly, this is the case with the Protagorean skill at rhetoric or "image" creation mentioned by Drucker. From Plato's point of view, e.g., the point of view of the *Charmides*, the equation of sophistry with the liberal arts deprives liberal arts education of the evaluative, critical, and integrating functions that are possible on the Socratic conception of the liberal arts. Moreover, since the sophistic master *technē* is rhetoric, tyranny, as Plato taught, is always lurking in the wings to substitute for statesmanship.[9]

Platonic liberal arts education is essential for a Platonic managerial statesman, for it helps to develop conceptual and synthetic skills—skills necessary to grasp the presuppositions and principles underlying a whole—as well as a humane business character. George Cabot Lodge is one of a number of management theorists who take a holistic (and a Platonic rather than sophistic) approach to management. He argues that in order to deal with the realities of contemporary business, a manager must be willing "to confront manifold change openly and with a breadth of vision.... He must see his task as a general not a specialized one.... He is an integrator, a synthesizer, responsible for the whole and capable of perceiving the whole, within and without."[10]

The search for comprehensive and interdisciplinary truths, the original goal of philosophy, is undermined by an overemphasis on specialization. Liberal arts education in the Socratic/Platonic tradition avoids this twentieth century emphasis. It manifests the spirit of ancient Greek education (*paideia*). *Paideia* involves the cultivation of the whole person, the development of a person's capacities or abilities; in this way, one can best respond to the challenges of life and live a happy life (*eudaimonia*). This view should be contrasted with a conception of education which makes technical or vocational instruction central.[11] If education is reduced to specialized training, the emphasis on technology and instrumental values would influence people to emphasize immediate practical concerns; technology would become people's master rather than slave and instrumental values would be elevated to the status of intrinsic values. From the standpoint of *paideia*, such a position, by limiting the development of both the human intellect and character, creates a myopic view of life, which makes one incapable of examining basic human values and thus living the good life. If we take the view of the ancient Greek philosophers (Socrates, Plato, and Aristotle) and attempt to understand the values that properly determine life as a whole, we must be open to these values; it is not enough to be a generalist in the sense of being a jack-of-all-intellectual-trades. There is a difference between being a lover of wisdom and a dilettante. In order to be open to values that are beneficial, we must understand the human soul and its proper education; this entails reflection on excellence (*aretē*)—excellence of character and intellectual excellence.

Drucker describes the management revolution in strictly instrumental terms. Applying managerial knowledge to knowledge, he says, should "produce results," should produce knowledge that is "needed," and should "make knowledge effective." He says that the management of knowledge is the new definition of management. If this is true, it is the definition of management as a technical or vocational skill, not the definition of a managerial statesman.[12] Managerial statesmanship requires Socratic *sōphrosynē.*

It is interesting to note that Drucker, in *The New Realities*—an earlier work than the one we are discussing—takes a Platonic rather than a sophistic view of the liberal arts. He says that management is a liberal art; it "deals with people, their values, their growth and development."[13] Thus, here, Drucker supports the view of ancient Greek *paideia.* He also emphasizes both the comprehensive and interdisciplinary nature of management.

> Management is ... what tradition used to call a liberal art—'liberal' because it deals with the fundamentals of knowledge, self-knowledge, wisdom and leadership; 'art' because it is practice and application. Managers draw on all the knowledges and insights of the humanities and the social sciences—on psychology and philosophy, on economics and history, on the physical sciences and ethics.[14]

Nonetheless, he does not develop this view, and in the work we are examining in this chapter, he seems to be moving away from it. In Section 1, we saw that Drucker recognizes that in a society peopled by specialists, questions of values, vision, and the nature of the educated person are of pressing importance. He also understands that a "universally educated person" in this knowledge society should resemble the traditional humanist because, as he suggests, such a society must deal with global issues and, therefore, requires what he calls a unifying force especially with respect to values. ("A common concept of excellence" and "mutual respect" pertain to values.) Yet, we saw that he believes that the traditional source of humanistic education, the classics, is insufficient—at least as it is practiced today—because its relevance to the present and future is unclear. I suggested that this relates to his view of a knowledge society as consisting of two tiers—of managers of organizations with specialized missions and of employees who are specialists within these organizations. Although it would be helpful for each of these two cultures (as he calls them) to experience one another, this, as I suggested, is insufficient to constitute liberality in the classical sense. How can these knowledges be integrated into a *"universe* of knowledge" by people who are specialists? Neither culture nurtures the Platonic dialectician—one who seeks knowledge of the good for the whole (society as a whole), and one who knows how to deal with problems relating to the whole. It may be possible for these two cultures to gain some mutual understanding of one another, but this is not a *"universe* of discourse." Discourse in such a universe would lack an essential ingredient—a Platonic type of discussion about ethical issues.

Drucker, himself, suggests an important aspect of the problem. As in Plato's *Republic,* organizations—like Plato's citizens and classes—according to Drucker, should stick to their peculiar functions. Since their functions are not directed to the whole, we saw that Drucker suggests that such specialists can only do harm to themselves and to society in positions where competence in dealing with the whole is necessary, e.g., in positions of political power. But instead of considering what I should think is a reasonable approach—the Platonic view—he seems to see no other alternative than to attempt to match the competencies of different organizations with social problems. But this solution is no solution because the *basic* social problems are beyond the competence of any of these specialists (or any combination of them). What makes his position worse is his belief that managers of these organizations (and possibly the specialists within the organizations) should believe that their task is "the most important ... in society." *Hubris* indeed! How can such myopic self-deception help in gaining a necessary holistic perspective? There is no "queen of the knowledges," he suggests, but by the consequences of his own position he seems to be forced in just this direction.

In conclusion, it is worth mentioning the following benefits of the Socratic/Platonic conception of the liberal arts that are applicable to

Drucker's knowledge society. Top business schools (as well as law schools) have emphasized the importance of the problem solving features of Socratic method. In the *Charmides*, the Platonic Socrates illustrates how, by means of Socratic method, he discovers problems and attempts to solve them. Second, helpful attitudes that liberal arts education can bring to business are often mentioned by proponents of the importance of the liberal arts to business—e.g., tolerance for ambiguity and complexity, lack of dogmatism and prejudice, curiosity and a love of learning. All of these attitudes are related to the foundational element of Socratic *sōphrosynē* or Socratic self-knowledge (discussed in Section 2), Socrates' humility. Socrates' questions directly attack interlocutors' dogmatism—their belief that they have knowledge when they are really ignorant. The intent of this questioning is to inspire the interlocutors to wonder and a love of learning; these notions are central to the philosophical attitude. Socratic questioning also forces interlocutors to come to grips with the complexities of value issues and to open up to opponent's points of view (rather than rationalizing their own pet positions). Socratic questioning is a training in liberalizing the mind by forcing it to be unprejudiced, that is, by forcing it to look for falsifying evidence for even our most treasured beliefs.

Notes

1. Peter F. Drucker, *Post-Capitalist Society* (New York: Harper Collins, 1993). References to this work (PCS) will be incorporated into the text and placed in parentheses.

2. Drucker is confused in arguing that Socrates radically separates *technē* from knowledge (the ability to do from the ability to know). In the *Charmides*, Plato grounds *technē* in knowledge (*epistēmē*). Indeed, it is because of this that one is able to understand the "general principles" underlying a *technē*, and a *technē* can be learned in a way other than by raw experience. The *Charmides* shows that *epistēmē* becomes even more important as a guide to *technē* when knowledge is of what is good and bad. Protagoras, on the other hand, as we shall see, deemphasizes knowledge in a Platonic sense and emphasizes rhetorical *technai* (pl. of *technē*) as practical guides. A difficult question which should be considered is whether or not the practical wisdom necessary for ethical business leadership is a type of technē? This question is discussed in Chapter 3.

3. Taylor showed "that work could be studied, analyzed, and divided into a series of simple repetitive motions—each of which had to be done in one right way, its own best time, and with the right tools" (PCS, 35).

4. Early in the dialogue, Socrates agrees, as a "physician," to cure Charmides's headache. However, a problem with the body requires attention to the body as a whole, and the body cannot be properly attended to without treating the soul—the soul as a whole. Problems with either the body or the soul will not be solved unless there is regard for the whole, and this requires attention to that which is good for the whole. Socrates' cure, Socratic method (dialectic), since it pertains to curing the soul (of its dogmatism) must be guided by considerations of good and bad. The intended result of Socratic method is Socratic *sōphrosynē* and the dialogue concludes with the necessity of connecting this virtue with knowledge of what is good and bad.

5. "Socratic Dialectic in the *Meno*," *Southern Journal of Philosophy*, vol. 24, #3 (Fall 1986): 351–363. "Mental Perception, Rational Justification in Inquiry, and Socratic Recollection in the *Meno*," *Dialogos*, #63 (1994): 75–99.

6. In the *Phaedo* (96a–99c), Socrates tells a story of how, when he was young, he had a passion for natural science and was puzzled about the causes of generation, corruption, and the preservation of existence. He became intrigued with Anaxagoras's doctrine that the mind (*nous*) causes and orders everything. However, he was disappointed to learn that Anaxagoras forsook mind for mechanical explanation. Could mechanical causes explain why Socrates chose to remain in prison rather than escape? Can *technai* explain how a system of technology can be ordered for the best—for what is best for society as a whole? Which of the *technai*, if any, has jurisdiction over the whole?

7. A case can be made for the view that Drucker's management works contain something like the Platonic notion of justice. A main theme in Drucker's management works is the notion that in a good organization, workers' strengths, not their weaknesses, are stressed. This emphasis on workers' strengths leads to Drucker's view that central to the good spirit of an organization, and therefore to proper business leadership, is that every effort be made to fit work to people's capacities. Typically, he says, "Organizing men for work ... means putting the man on the job he will do best" [Peter F. Drucker, *The Practice of Management* (New York: Harpers Row, 1954), p. 299]. When Drucker speaks with this voice, his notion of leadership has a distinct Platonic flavor. In a recent work by the Drucker Foundation [*Leader to Leader*, eds., Francis Hesselbein and Paul M. Cohen (San Francisco: Jossey-Bass Pubs., 1999)], Max De Pree, Chairman and CEO of Herman Miller, relates Drucker's thesis concerning emphasis on workers' strengths to the notion that there is a common good in which ideally we should participate by having tasks dispersed in accordance with our strengths ("gifts"). The implicit concept of leadership is clearly Platonic. He tells us that at Herman Miller, "We had a community of people who got to be as good as they could be because we were

able to sort out their gifts and assign tasks according to those gifts" (p. 160). Moreover, a recurrent theme in this work is the importance of self-knowledge to business leadership. According to De Pree, one cannot get an organization's house in order until one gets one's personal house (soul) in order. He says that "It is tough to follow somebody who doesn't have that sense of himself" (p. 19). James M. Kouzes, chairman of Tom Peters Group Learning Systems, places what one represents or who one is at the center of leadership. Self-knowledge and the integrity that results from acting from self-knowledge, as Socrates shows, is central to leadership. Thus Kouzes says, "People don't follow your technique. They follow you—your message and your embodiment of that message" (p. 39). Peter M. Singer discusses the cynicism that results from mission or purpose statements that have not transformed the organization to manifest them. The soul of such an organization is hypocritical; it lacks integrity and its leaders are either hypocritical, lacking in self-knowledge or both. Leadership involves the acceptance of its burdens and this requires management of the stresses that pertain to leadership. Linda A. Hill says, "To be effective in handling the stresses of leading others, people have to learn a great deal about themselves–their personal values, styles, strengths, and weaknesses" (p. 294).

8.　The other great sophist of Protagoras's generation, Gorgias, saw skill in *logoi* as the road to power. Plato criticizes Gorgias's art in the same way in which he criticizes the rhetoric of Protagoras—it is morally neutral, pertaining to means and not ends. The practice was defended by a relativistic philosophy similar to that of Protagoras.

9.　Scott Buchanan ["Natural Law and Teleology," in *Natural Law and Modern Society* (Cleveland: The World Publishing Company, 1962)] calls Plato "the researcher in Greek technology." "He is concerned to get the whole technology in a single view, and it results in the end in seeing politics, the art of government, as the master art which as end gives order to all the other arts; hence also to the classes and virtues of men" (pp. 84–85). Buchanan continues, "If we look at all of our occupations as elementary units of a unified, highly organized industrial system, we are struck with the possibility that some dictatorial managerial bureaucracy could take over and with scientific and engineering know-how could exploit the system for almost any arbitrary purpose" (p. 85), and the same comment can be made about Drucker's knowledge society. The sophist, as distinct from Plato's statesman, is a prime candidate for such a tyrant. As Buchanan says, "The sophist was for Plato the prototype of the tyrant. With his sophisticated expertise, his claim of omniscience, his obvious hunger for power, and his hard salesmanship, he imitates and caricatures government" (pp. 85–86).

10.　George C. Lodge, "Business and the Changing Society," in *Issues in Business and Society*, eds. George A. Steiner and John F. Steiner, 2nd ed. (New York: Random House, 1977), p. 144.

11. Plato refuses to distinguish sharply between ethical and nonethical realms of activity. One should be fundamentally concerned with the excellence of the whole of one's life, of which one's career is a part. Human excellences or virtues should be manifest in our lives and not merely in circumscribed parts of our lives. One important consequence of this is the benefit of the virtuous person to society. His or her generosity is not a part of one's life, e.g., the occasional gift giver or philanthropist, it is a consequence of living the good life.

12. The terms "managerial statesman" and "managerial statesmanship," as I use them, imply ethical leadership.

13. Peter F. Drucker, *The New Realities* (New York: Harper and Row, 1989), p. 231.

14. Drucker, p. 231. In a recent book on Drucker [Peter Drucker: *Shaping The Managerial Mind* (San Francisco: Jossey-Bass Publishers, 1999)], John E. Flaherty maintains that "[Drucker] never ceased to consider liberal arts to be the heart and soul of the managerial process. His untutored exploration into the classics as a young man later convinced him that without the liberal arts, management would degenerate into a bloodless and inanimate subject" (p. 7). Moreover, not only does Flaherty mention the interdisciplinary nature of Drucker's own knowledge—including the subjects mentioned in this quotation—he correctly notes that Drucker's book, *The Practice of Management* "synthesized the best of current practice into codified principles … [and] integrated the specialized business functions into an organic whole" (p. 112). Flaherty suggests that Drucker's originality in this book "consisted in merging the key specialties into a holistic perspective" (p. 112).

CHAPTER II

Don Quixote and the Problem of Idealism and Realism in Business Ethics

Introduction

In his introduction to *Business as a Humanity*, Thomas J. Donaldson says that the authors of this volume agree that humanities' texts, e.g., philosophical, historical, and literary works, should be assigned in business schools.[1] Business ethicists have shown the importance of philosophical and historical research in business ethics. Possibly, however, not enough has been said about the importance of literature in business ethics. .

In his *Business as a Humanity: A Contradiction in Terms?* Richard T. De George maintains that literature offers the business student

> subtlety of insight, beauty of language, imagination, and vivid description that puts most texts to shame.... [Students] do need to understand people and their motives, to know how to read and judge character, and to have the ability to imagine themselves in another's shoes, be they those of a competitor, a boss, or a subordinate. For those dedicated to the case method, novels, short stories, and plays offer an inexhaustible storehouse of riches, more detailed, subtle, and complete than most cases written up for courses.[2]

In this chapter, I am not concerned with the use of literature in case studies, although I agree with De George about its usefulness. I am more interested in how great literature increases our insight, broadens our imagination, and helps us to get beyond surface judgments so as to further mutual understanding and sympathy, i.e., that which helps us to imagine ourselves "in another's shoes." I shall limit myself to a discussion of one work of literature—but certainly one of the greatest—*Don Quixote*. In discussing *Don Quixote*, I also have a more specific purpose in mind which relates this chapter to the previous one.

In the previous chapter, Socrates raises the question of the impracticality of Socratic philosophy or Socratic dialectic. We saw that Drucker notes that the present generation questions the practical value of a related notion of the liberal arts. I defended the Socratic model of ethical leadership (the philosopher king as statesman)—which entails Socratic dialectic, knowledge of the good, and the liberal arts—against the claims of specialists who might argue that it is too impractical. In this chapter, I revisit the problem of the practicality of an idealistic model of ethical leadership. *Don Quixote* is used to consider the place of idealistic theory and realistic practice[3] in business ethics. In my discussion of ethical business leadership, I attempt to create a useful model of this concept—what I call a quixotified Sancho Panza—by blending theoretical idealism and practical realism.

Idealism, Realism, and *Don Quixote*

The danger of separating idealistic theory from realistic practice is a central issue for Miguel De Cervantes in *Don Quixote*. Cervantes condemns the books of chivalry, as embodied in his character Don Quixote, as both fantastic and dangerous. The chivalric hero may seduce people into believing that the improbable can be achieved with ease.[4] Cervantes's character, Don Quixote, shows that this is not the case. Here is a hero possessed of fine qualities of both character and intellect who sallies forth in the name of justice and human betterment. Nonetheless, while being inspired by high ideals, his efforts are futile because he pays little or no attention to the means necessary for achieving these ends, and he fails to gain requisite knowledge of the circumstances and conditions necessary to properly understand human actions. Cervantes seems to be saying that when idealistic theory is divorced from practice, however noble the theory and good the intentions, requisite skill, judgment, and discretion will be lacking and the human good will not be advanced. People who neglect practical experience for idealistic theory are not practically wise; they often apply principles recklessly to people and situations. This is illustrated in the character, Don Quixote. Obsessed with a theory (of doing good) and convinced that it is his duty to interfere in other people's lives, Don Quixote's utopianism reeks havoc on those people with whom he has contact, for he is careless and inconsiderate in applying his theory. In an early adventure, he attempts to impose his ideal on some merchants he chances to meet; he insists that they admit that Dulcinea is the most beautiful of women. The merchants want evidence of her beauty, but he attempts to force them to admit it with painful results to himself. His misperception of people—a result of his runaway idealism—also has painful consequences. In the adventure with the King's prisoners, he frees them and expects gratitude in return—that they sing the praises of Dulcinea. Instead, he is subjected to the prisoners' ingratitude; he is stoned and beaten by them.

But the consequences for others are also painful. Don Quixote presents himself as an authority on the administration of justice. But in not minding his own business, although he thinks that what he does is his business, he harms people, people who are often innocent. What he calls adventures, then, are often misadventures for others. As a servant who was unfortunate enough to be "helped" by Don Quixote says, "I do not know what you mean by righting wrongs, seeing that you found me quite all right and left me very wrong indeed, with a broken leg which will not be right again as long as I live."[5] "No misfortune," says the servant, "could be so great as that which comes of being helped by you."[6]

It would seem, then, that Cervantes creates Don Quixote as a well-intentioned but ludicrous utopian. His ideal fictions are more real to him than anything he experiences in the world. This is, in part, caused by Don Quixote living in books (of chivalry) rather than in the real world. Indeed, he seems to be created as an oxymoron—a bookish knight. He yearns to serve mankind and bring honor and glory to himself, but he seems to fail on both counts. Don Quixote fits himself with an old suit of armor, a makeshift helmet, and a nag to sally forth for what is right and good, but he is obviously ill-equipped. His idealism is so divorced from reality that to him nothing is what it appears to be. His chivalric imagination transforms everything into something wondrous or beautiful; a windmill is a giant, sheep are armies, a run down inn is a castle, wenches are ladies, a thieving innkeeper is the governor of a castle, etc.

Irving Kristol's article, "Utopianism, Ancient and Modern,"[7] could have been written (but was not) with Don Quixote in mind. He says that "Men are dreaming animals and the incapacity to dream makes a man less than human."[8] The human imagination, in its creativity, envisions various forms of perfection. According to Kristol, this is positive. However, "there are also madmen who find it impossible to disentangle dreams from reality—and this kind of madness we have had, alas, far too much experience."[9] He calls this inability to distinguish political dreams from reality "utopianism."[10] He suggests that Plato understands this distinction, for he says that his utopia was designed to produce "better political philosophers, not better politics."[11] Kristol, I think, is too pessimistic about the possibility of applying idealistic political philosophy to political realities. I shall consider the parallel problem of applying idealistic theory to business in the final section of this chapter.

So far our Don Quixote scenario could provide a cautionary tale for business ethics. Some businesspeople with a good deal of practical experience have looked askance at the sallies of philosophical bookish knights armed with their (e.g., deontological and/or utilitarian) moral theories, which they learned "living in books."[12] They might argue that there is something comic in some philosophers' attempts to help business leaders solve morally complex business problems by applying moral theories to overly simplified "case studies." Although business ethics philosophers are not necessarily naive about the practical complexities of business and some businesspeople's notion of practicality is too myopic and concrete, there appears to be some truth to the above complaint. In all events, there are businesspeople and business academics who perceive the works of business ethics philosophers as too vague, abstract, and theoretical, and generally too removed from the realities of business life to do much good. Thus, like Don Quixote, these philosophers are seen to be ill-equipped for their task.

But Don Quixote's misapplied idealism and his putative confusion of appearance and reality is only a part of the story. As we laugh at this person who wants to be a hero but seems to be ill-equipped to be one—he is certainly the reverse of a young, handsome, and dashing romantic hero—we also feel sadness. As we reflect on this, we realize that his nobility, his courage and virtue in general, his endurance and optimism in the face of repeated failures are real; even admitting the improbability of his ideals, he himself is the embodiment of these ideals, and he expresses them quite eloquently.[13] Moreover, why not think that in an age full of depravity, "knight errantry" is necessary to remedy evils and help the needy? As Don Quixote says, the deceivers have made the things of great worth appear to be worthless.[14]

People who meet Don Quixote often treat him as insane (especially in the first part of the work) but not Sancho Panza. Is it so strange to say, as Don Quixote says, that there are deceivers (enchanters) continually trying to deceive us into thinking that appearances are reality? Cervantes is known for his love of truth and justice and so is his character, Don Quixote. But the world does not necessarily embody such love. External appearances are deceptive. Characters in *Don Quixote* exhibit dishonesty, deceit, fraud, corruption, and every known vice; truth is also distorted by human passions, wealth, love of reputation, gossip, and the like. No wonder, as Cervantes seems to be saying, truth is illusive. But if there is a dark truth consistent with human pessimism, should we not be allowed to dream of a light truth consistent with human optimism? If we are to take seriously Niccolo Machiavelli and Thomas Hobbes when doing business ethics, should we not also give careful consideration to Cervantes?[15]

Don Quixote, as Benedetto Croce says, inspires *simpatia* in readers—"recognition of something which is identified with what we ourselves honor and cherish."[16] Although there are people who misunderstand and dislike Don Quixote, decent people all like him. Even Sancho Panza, who desires wealth and power and is described as somewhat roguish, can transcend these worldly desires by his love and admiration for Don Quixote. People throughout the ages have endorsed Sancho's sentiment, for a belief in a reality of what is hoped for is basic to the human spirit. Croce says, "From time to time we all suffer the sorrow of having dreamed and trusted, only to face cruel awakening and disillusionment. This is the price paid for life by even the most noble and expert, the most austere and wary."[17] "But," Croce continues, "beyond appearances, there is in the midst of illusion true reality, the reality of the ideal which makes us live and work, the ideal for which we suffer and die."[18]

Don Quixote distinguishes between knights that are courtiers and knights-errant. The former are protected against the negative experiences of the real world by the protection of the court. Knights-errant, on the other hand, must face every conceivable danger with "highborn mien and intrepid heart."[19] This is consistent with what Croce says, but for knights-errant to be effective, they cannot ignore the practical realities of life, as we have seen Don Quixote often does. Thus Cervantes cannot let the matter rest with his hero's idealism. He attempts to show how this idealism may be effective, and to this end, Sancho Panza is necessary.

Don Quixote and Sancho Panza, the two main characters of the novel, are quite different from one another. The former is a tall, emaciated, fastidious, well-educated, spirited idealist while the latter is a plump, squat, uneducated, timid, practical realist. Don Quixote convinces Sancho Panza, a poor farmer, to be his squire by promising him the governorship of an island. Sancho initially follows Don Quixote in the hope of wealth and adventure as well as power. But in a touching passage, Sancho explains more fully why he follows Don Quixote. He says, "We're from the same village, I've eaten his bread, I like him very much, he's generous to me, he gave me his ass-colts, and above all, I'm loyal; and so it's impossible for anything to separate us except pick and spade."[20] In their constant interaction, driven by dialogue, they grow to understand each other; indeed, they like each other and need one another's company. It is often remarked that the great strength of this novel is the slow development of these two characters. The development is as much due to their mutual interactions as it is to their experiences. In reacting to one another, they become more like one another. This central feature of the novel can serve as a model for discovering a mean between two extremes: the idealistic moral philosopher (often armed with the tools of the deontologist and/or utilitarian) who comes down from his or her vision of the good into Plato's cave to save business from its moral evils and the so-called practical businessperson who sees no value in ideals since he or she believes they do not serve to benefit the bottom line, and generally have no place in business or, at best, only a marginal place.

Let us consider more fully the interaction and development of our two characters. Early in the novel Sancho is unwilling to accept our hero's perceptions, e.g., windmills are giants and sheep are armies. But Don Quixote is able to seduce Sancho by spinning the most outlandishly romantic yarns in which the knight and his squire fulfill their desires. Slowly Sancho accepts some of Don Quixote's perceptions. To him, Don Quixote is often foolhardy, but he is not insane. Although Sancho is influenced by our hero, he is also his own man and questions his "master." When Don Quixote is put into a cage in order to be taken home and cured, Sancho disagrees with our hero's view that he is being bewitched by enchanters, and Sancho is correct. Sancho recognizes that his "master" is quite complex. He wonders how a person who can say as many wise things as Don Quixote says can also believe in the nonsensical and impossible, e.g., the tale of the cave of Montesinos. This ambivalence is also reflected in his relation of squire to Don Quixote. He often, in his pain, expresses regret at having followed our hero, but on reflection he recants. He learns that, like his master, what supports him is faith and trust. But our hero also learns this lesson the hard way, with pain. He progresses from trying to force people to accept the "truth" that his Dulcinea is the most beautiful of women to saying that "God knows whether or not there is a Dulcinea in this world or if she is a fanciful creation."[21] Moreover, he learns that Sancho is also complex. He tells us that although Sancho blunders and appears simple minded, he is also sharp-witted. "He doubts everything and believes everything, and just as I think he is about to tumble headlong, owing to some stupidity, he will come up with some witticism or other that sends him skyward in my estimation."[22]

This complex relationship between two complex but very different persons is fed by a dialectic in which the primary ingredients are idealism and common sense realism. As we progress from chapter to chapter and adventure to adventure, we notice that the relationship between our two characters deepens and so does their understanding of one another.

Without Don Quixote, Sancho may well have been only a practical, crafty, materialistic peasant. Instead, toward the end of the novel, he rises to a higher level; be becomes a wise ruler, exhibiting the judgment, discretion, and power of expression of a fine statesman. Indeed, Sancho has so assimilated our hero's ideals that he says that the most pleasant thing is to be "a respected man, squire to a knight-errant who goes in search of adventures."[23] Without Sancho Panza, on the other hand, Don Quixote may well have remained an airy idealist. Sancho helps to temper our hero's foolhardiness or rashness; his sense of courage becomes much more Aristotelian or moderate. Don Quixote says, "I would have you know, Sancho, that valor not based upon prudence can only be termed temerity, and the triumphs of the foolhardy are to be attributed to good luck rather than to courage."[24] But the position that Don Quixote is criticizing is that of a nonsanchofied Don Quixote. It is also possible that under Sancho's influence, he is more capable of learning practical lessons. In the episode with the knight of the mirrors, he suggests that he has been taught "to restrain and moderate the impetuosity of my wrath and make a gentle use of my glorious victory."[25] Moreover, he learns to identify things more accurately; some things are what they seem to be—sometimes an inn is identified as an inn, a puppet show as a puppet show, and later in the novel, although he has reason to transform a country girl into Dulcinea, he does not do it.

At the beginning of this chapter, I suggested that De George is right in emphasizing that great literature increases our insight, broadens our imagination, and furthers mutual understanding and sympathy. *Don Quixote* is as good an example of such benefits of literature as one can find. If idealistic business ethics theoreticians are at odds with the more empirical minded common sense business realists, would they not both benefit from reading *Don Quixote*? Indeed, Cervantes's delineation of the characters of Don Quixote and Sancho Panza and their mutual influence on one another may well serve as a model of how mutual understanding and sympathy, increased insight, and broadened perspectives are possible if idealistic theoreticians and common sense realists are willing to "live" and work together in the common pursuit of what is honorable and high-minded in business. We saw that Cervantes tells us that fiction should be written so that the impossible is made to appear possible. Cervantes creates an experience, so to speak, of two opposite types of people influencing one another, growing together, and learning to admire and love one another. We are able, then, to *imagine* how what may have seemed to be impossible is possible and thus provide hope for a real and fruitful dialogue between people with radically different philosophies who write in the field of business ethics or are involved in one way or another with business.

A Quixotified Sancho as Statesman

Don Quixote never becomes a ruler; however, Sancho Panza wants to become a ruler and does. A major cause of Sancho's statesmanlike wisdom is his interaction with Don Quixote. This suggests a possible solution to a problem in managerial statesmanship. Cervantes apparently never believed that Don Quixote would be accepted as a political leader. Evidently, people will not welcome an idealistic theoretician as ruler. A person who is practical and realistic would be more readily accepted. It seems that one must combine the idealism and wisdom of Don Quixote and the realism and practicality of Sancho Panza. If Sancho would be considered a more suitable ruler than Don Quixote, what is necessary, as Cervantes suggests, is for Don Quixote to educate Sancho Panza—to nurture a quixotified Sancho. Actually, we saw that Cervantes views the interaction of Don Quixote and Sancho Panza as one of mutual influence for the betterment of both of his heros.[26] Cervantes's model may well prove useful in understanding ethical business leadership. However, since a quixotified Sancho Panza and not Don Quixote himself seems to represent the best hope of properly combining theoretical idealism and practical realism in one managerial statesman, the following question must be addressed: Will business accept a quixotified Sancho Panza?[27] In what follows, I shall discuss both negative and positive answers to this question. In Section 4, I shall consider authors who offer some evidence for the position that quixotic idealism has little chance of being implemented in business practice. In Section 5, I attempt to show how a quixotic ideal can be realized in business.

A Quixotified Sancho as Managerial Statesman: A Negative View

Postdepression American business has been influenced by values central to the functioning of formal organizations. The most famous of such values are those attributed to the organization man. The ethic of the organization man, which William H. Whyte, Jr. calls the social ethic,[28] emphasizes the concepts of belongingness (emotional security and stability generated by effecting total integration into an organization) and togetherness (teamwork, committee work and the like as basic to decision making) rather than individual judgment.

The more extreme form of organization man is the true believer who sacrifices real virtue for the avoidance of the pain of moral conflict and moral search, and his extreme bureaucratic tendencies make this ethic, at its worst, repressive, lacking in idealism, insensitive, and destructive of the individual. Generally, the conformist values of the organization man tend to erode our courage and integrity and force moral decisions into a conventional mode—one governed by majority opinion and motivated by fear and concern for external rewards. Their morality is reduced to a superficial concern with manners, but there is no real commitment to self-development or to anything that gives quality to life.

In *The Gamesman*, Michael Maccoby argues that although the organization (company) man still exists, the gamesman, who seems to be a combination of the organization man and the robber baron, is the most dominant upper echelon management type. Nonetheless, a generally shallow morality involving a lack of concern for others and a want of idealism, according to Maccoby, is typical of gamesmen and therefore of modern corporate leadership. In a popular chapter of *The Gamesman*, "The Heart and the Head," Maccoby suggests that corporations emphasize mental attributes such as problem solving skills, as those essential for work, rather than what he calls "qualities of the heart"—moral qualities—e.g., empathy, compassion, generosity, and idealism.[29] "Tough-minded realistic thought" is opposed to "softness, feeling, and generosity."[30]

Careerism, which he calls "the modern pathology of the heart," is the principal cause of the undeveloped heart in what he believes to be the preferred business leader—the gamesman. The careerist cannot afford "idealistic, compassionate, and courageous impulses that might jeopardize his career."[31] In order to gain career goals, the careerist shields himself or herself from empathic feelings, compassion, and generally from social responsibilities; in Maccoby's terms, he "builds a shell around the heart."[32]

A similarly depressing view is presented in William Scott and David Hart's update of Whyte's *Organization Man*. Virtue, they argue, does not triumph in the modern organization; what triumphs is "organizational stagnation, the spoiling of idealism, official insensitivity, despotic repression, and the blighting of human aspirations."[33]

A number of contemporary business analysts support Maccoby's position, but attribute the "heartlessness" of American business organizations to their bureaucratic nature.[34] Roger D'Aprix laments the bureaucratic nature of corporations. The satisfaction of human needs are subordinated to the well-being and the survival of the organization. He supports the view of Margaret Henning. Corporate life stultifies our feelings and creates "an environment in which the basic affections of human beings are primarily taboo. It is a climate in which love is not allowed ..., kindness is devalued ..., [and a] concern for people is called 'soft.'"[35]

Robert Jackall supports Maccoby's view and again attributes the heartlessness of the modern corporation to its bureaucratic nature. Since activities are compartmentalized in bureaucracies, managers often do not perceive, or are not concerned with, problems relating to segments of the whole larger than their own. The narrowing of one's moral vistas involves a hardening of the heart. "The managerial world," he says, "is not notable for its compassion."[36] Heartlessness is buttressed by an emphasis on the goals of personal ambition and survival—a point mentioned by many analysts of business. These goals tend to lead to the view that the bureaucratic terrain is a battlefield and the warriors are divided into winners and losers. One must then forsake moral qualities, in this zero-sum game, for whatever effectively results in survival and success. The stress on success devalues friendships and reduces them to relationships of expediency. Jackall echoes the complaint made by Scott, Hart and many others that bureaucracies emphasize expediency. Therefore moral issues are not considered; what is considered is that which is consistent with "institutional logic and of advantage to oneself and to one's social network."[37] Bureaucratic leaders effectively insulate themselves from moral issues, which must be dealt with by pushing them down the hierarchy of the firm, forcing their underlings to deal with the dirty work.[38] Moreover, moral qualities cannot thrive in a world dominated by appearances. But this, according to Jackall and others, characterizes the world of formal organizations. Stress is on managing appearances, masking intentions, controlling one's emotions, and mastering the necessary "public faces."[39]

It is difficult to see how a quixotified Sancho can practice managerial statesmanship in this environment. But such managerial statesmanship will also be absent in a business environment that overemphasizes economics.

Leonard Silk, David Vogel and others have argued that the more myopic business leaders still refuse to see corporate business as something more than an economic institution. They hold what has been called the classical view of business (business has no social responsibilities other than to produce goods and services efficiently, make money for shareholders, and conduct business in a lawful manner).[40] Silk and Vogel (in the executive conferences they held), maintain that "the classical strain seemed dominant" among corporate executives.[41]

Silk and Vogel claim that "most businessmen project their own special perspective on society at large; for them, the world is seen essentially as a marketplace, and the overriding objective of virtually everyone is considered to be personal gain."[42] Kristol argues that this view, although traditional, is unacceptable given the power and impact of corporations on society. Because of this impact, they are expected to attend to the public interest.[43] Moreover, George C. Lodge argues that the overemphasis on purely economic matters, by business leaders, is a symptom of adhering to an anachronistic ideology ("a framework of ideas which a community uses to define values and to make them explicit").[44]

E. F. Schumacher suggests that the financier is the preferred type of corporate leader because business overemphasizes economic values. This leader transforms noneconomic values, by the method of cost/benefit analysis, into economic values.[45] This will not be done out of a "bad heart"; it will be a product of an ignorance of what is required by the corporation as a whole and a consequence of putting a specialist, rather than a qualified generalist, in the position of running an operation. A quixotified Sancho will not survive in this environment.

What about the 1990s? S. Prakash Sethi says, "While the 1980s were condemned as the decade of corporate greed, the 1990s are emerging as the decade of the heartless corporation."[46] He reminds us that corporations such as IBM, which were the opposite of heartless, were forced to radically downsize due to global competition, changing technologies, and a communication revolution. Will an injection of moral idealism help? Do corporations need a quixotified Sancho Panza? Sethi says, "Those who put their naive faith in the idea that corporations can do well by doing good, i.e., good ethics is always good business, are either assuming away the market advantages that these companies hold or refusing to accept history as it exists and substituting instead their perception of reality as what it ought to be."[47]

In "The Pain of Downsizing," John A. Byrne calls downsizing "a central fact of corporate life in the 1990s."[48] He chronicles the bitterness and lack of morale among managers at many firms that have radically downsized.[49] Euphemisms such as "reengineering" merely hide its painful human consequences. Although a number of prominent executives argue that downsizing of large corporations is necessary to maintain competitiveness in fast-changing global markets, many managers believe that they have been sacrificed to the bottom line. One may also add that while the economic indicators were up, real wages were stagnant and income distribution became more unequal in the 1990s. Byrne suggests that "Today's corporation is no longer a secure or stable place. It's an uncertain, turbulent environment where managers often find their compassion and humanity in conflict with the pressures of competition and ambition."[50] Whatever the putative benefits with respect to productivity, breaking up bureaucracies, and willingness to take risks are, this recent business trend does not create an environment in which a quixotified Sancho Panza can thrive.

A Quixotified Sancho as Managerial Statesman: A Positive View

Thomas J. Peters and Robert H. Waterman, Jr. suggest the importance of the quixotic element in our lives when they say, "We desperately need meaning in our lives and will sacrifice a great deal to institutions that will provide meaning for us."[51] Sancho-type motivations are further indicated when they suggest that this desire to find meaning is coupled with a desire to "transcend mundane things."[52] Moreover, this passion to find meaning in our lives involves going beyond a world of illusion created by "a conspiracy of the senses" to "fairy tales" and "myths."[53] Peters and Waterman suggest that a type of business leadership called "transforming leadership"—a term coined by James MacGregor Burns—builds upon this need to find meaning by creating a culture in which the guiding values can inspire employees.[54] One is reminded of Croce's notion of *simpatia*, which he uses to explain the effect of Don Quixote on readers. In a statement reminiscent of the relationship between Don Quixote and Sancho Panza, Peters and Waterman, quoting James MacGregor Burns, say, "[Transforming leadership] occurs when one or more persons *engage* with others in such a way that leaders and followers raise one another to higher levels of motivation and morality."[55] The following description of transforming leadership by Burns could have been written with *Don Quixote* in mind; it is an excellent statement of the relationship between Don Quixote and Sancho Panza. "The transforming leader looks for potential motives in followers, seeks to satisfy higher needs, and engages the full person of the follower. The result of transforming leadership is a relationship of mutual stimulation and elevation that converts followers into leaders and may convert leaders into moral agents."[56]

Peters and Waterman maintain that transforming leaders use the "language of uplift and idealism" to create myths that embody a corporation's values; that is, such myths "contribute to the unified sense of mission and thereby to the harmony of the whole."[57] Thus, like Don Quixote, the transforming leader is concerned with "soaring, lofty visions that will generate excitement and enthusiasm," and these values, embodied in a mythology, are instilled "through deeds rather than words."[58] Moreover, as is the case with Don Quixote, persistence is necessary if one is to have a chance of instilling quixotic values.[59] Transforming leaders, however, do not exhibit Don Quixote's tragic flaw, i.e., inattention to practice so that requisite means and knowledge for achieving ideals are neglected. Peters and Waterman tell us that "an effective leader must be the master of two ends of the spectrum: ideas at the highest level of abstraction and actions at the most mundane level of detail."[60] Thus, along with "soaring, lofty visions" this leader is "a bug for details" and, therefore, pays as much attention to what is necessary for implementing ideals as he does to the ideals themselves.[61] I now turn to more recent discussions of leadership insofar as they relate to the concept of a quixotified Sancho Panza.

Combining vision and practicality has been emphasized recently by Ronald A. Heifetz. He analyzes four traditional approaches to so-called objective leadership that purport to be value free. He says, "When defining leadership in terms of prominence, authority, and influence, however, these theories introduce value-biases implicitly without declaring their introduction...."[62] Leadership, he thinks, should have a value orientation directed toward social goods. Yet proper leadership must also be practical or what he calls adaptive. "Adaptive work consists of the learning required to address conflicts in the values people hold, or to diminish the gap between the values people stand for and the reality they face."[63] Central to such a task is the balancing of conflicting interests. Don Quixote and Sancho Panza, it seems, must be connected. Heifetz believes that proper adaptive leadership requires vision, but it is also action oriented. Heifetz says, "Just as clarifying a vision demands reality testing, reality testing is not a value-free process. Values are shaped and refined by rubbing against real problems, and people interpret their problems according to the values they hold."[64]

Warren Bennis echos the complaints of authors discussed in the previous section. He laments the moral dangers of leadership by organization people, a generation devoted to greed and excessive individualism, and the amorality of corporate bureaucracies.[65] Such visionless leaders ironically think that they are the realists when in fact they are out of touch with the world. However, in *On Becoming A Leader*, Bennis proposes what we have called a quixotified Sancho Panza as the proper leader for "forging a new future" instead of denying the possibility of such a leader. "*Leaders manage the dream. All leaders have* the capacity to create a compelling vision, one that takes people to a new place, and then translate that vision into reality."[66] Bennis says that his study of leadership shows that "true leaders" have integrity and have identified their "true calling"; they fulfill "their own genius, their visions of excellence, through the application of passion, energy, and focus."[67] In recalling their own vision, they help employees to do the same. Leaders who succeed emphasize imagination rather than obedience. Bennis says, "One of the greatest threats to American business, perhaps the ultimate threat, is its narrowing of horizons, its tendency to restrict its vision and devote its principal energies to just hanging in there...."[68]

Similarly, Noel M. Tichy and Mary Anne Devanna suggest that "one of the basic problems that we encounter in organizations is that it is culturally illegitimate to fantasize and dream about the future. If the idea cannot be presented in great rational detail it is dismissed as a half-baked scheme."[69] Yet, they suggest that such a quixotic quality is essential for business and is provided by transformational leaders; they provide the vision.[70]

Burt Nanus, however, reminds us that idealistic vision must be married to practical effectiveness. Nanus suggests the connection between leadership and a quixotified Sancho Panza. "Leaders take charge, make things happen, dream dreams and then translate them into reality. Leaders attract the voluntary commitment of followers, energize them, and transform organizations into new entities with greater potential for survival, growth and excellence."[71] The quixotic element is particularly well captured in the following: "Progress in organizations, like all human progress, is driven by the idealism and optimism captured in a persuasive and appealing vision of the future."[72]

What Nanus calls "powerful and transforming visions" must, then, as he suggests, be both idealistic—and therefore ambitious—and practical. They embody high standards (ideals) of excellence. The vision, which provides purpose and direction, should be clearly articulated, and it should tap into the needs and aspirations of stakeholders; the ideal must also be realistic. Given the organization's culture and values, it should express what is practically possible for that organization in the future.[73]

The qualities that Bennis, Tichy, and Devanna, for example, attribute to true leaders are the qualities, in the main, that Cervantes would applaud in a leader. True leadership, according to Bennis in *Why Leaders Can't Lead*, is based upon virtue—integrity (moral and intellectual honesty and willingness to act on principle), humility, dedication, magnanimity (noble mind and heart), openness, and creativity. In *On Becoming a Leader*, his list includes the following: Guiding vision, passion, integrity (self-knowledge, candor, and maturity), trust as a product of leadership, curiosity, and daring. Tichy and Devanna's list of the characteristics of a transformational leader again highlights the importance of a quixotified Sancho Panza. They are change agents, courageous, believe in people's potentials, are value-driven, life-long learners, have the ability to deal with complexity, ambiguity, and uncertainty, and are visionaries.[74]

It is clear from what has been said that a number of writers on leadership would agree with the concept of a quixotified Sancho Panza. In our context, however, it is most important to develop the ethical implications of this model for business. What helps to make a quixotic business vision ethical, and what is its content? In what follows, I shall develop one of a number of possibilities.

Bennis suggests that a practical leader's vision should be deeply rooted in human needs; this will at least give it staying power. A concern for quality—which he suggests has been lacking in "modern industrial society"—and, linked to quality, a dedication and love of our work, he insists is essential to the vision.[75] Similarly, Nanus believes that the right vision must inspire "excellence and achievement in organizations."[76] Tichy, Devanna, Badaracco, and Ellsworth underscore the importance of leaders believing in persons' potentials or in their latent abilities.

Badaracco and Ellsworth maintain that "outstanding performance will come from the 'hearts and mind' of employees attracted and motivated by higher values. The leader's job [as a quixotified Sancho Panza] is to harness people's deep needs and aspirations,"[77] as Bennis suggests. What are these needs and aspirations? In a section entitled "why is leadership rare"? they suggest that many people enter corporations with leadership attributes such as drive, energy, and ideas only to be beaten down by "bureaucratic processes, political infighting, and the erosive pressure of day-to-day problems."[78] However, they believe that the fault lies often with these persons' false view of human behavior. "We have inadequate faith in the abilities of others or we view human motivation only in terms of the self-interested pursuit of power, money, and security. We fail to recognize that people are also motivated by a need to create and a desire to serve worthwhile ends."[79] These authors, then, are offering a Cervantian answer to the problem of the rarity of leadership. Indeed, they continue in a Cervantian vein. What is lacking, they suggest, is "the courage to do and say what one believes to be right ...; the courage to act on one's vision for his or her organization."[80]

An emphasis on the pursuit of excellence was popularized in the early 80s by Peters and Waterman. They insist that business should emphasize quality goods and services rather than short term profits. They, like many other critics of business, blame business managers for overemphasizing finance and, generally, short term bottom line concerns.[81] Human beings are quite willing, if given the chance, to dedicate themselves to values one might consider noble. Indeed, they argue that the more successful firms are capable of motivating employees by "beautiful goals." They emphasize quality and reliable products and services and concern for people. In general, excellent companies create environments in which employees can develop their abilities (and gain personal satisfaction and pride in their accomplishments) and be treated with respect and dignity.[82] I have called this the ideal of craftsmanship.[83]

The ideal of craftsmanship is to create that which has quality or excellence; personal satisfaction, pride in accomplishment, and a sense of dignity derived from the consequent self-development are the motivations. In an "excellent" company, it is this ideal that permeates the firm, and management should provide the moral example of such an ideal; a business management craftsman attempts to create a quality organization, and quality products and services are the result of such an organization.[84]

Such management accords with a conception of justice which takes seriously the concept of corporate stakeholders. Not only will shareholders benefit from such an "excellent" company, so will the workers who "get their due," and the consumers who get quality and reliable products and services. Such business management will not be myopically dominated by the bottom line. In general, the skepticism concerning a quixotified Sancho as managerial statesman, which permeates the discussion in the previous section can be undermined if managers would take seriously what might be called the craftsmanship ethic.

Tom Peters, who has changed his mind about a number of things written in his 1982 work (especially about the celebration of big manufacturing businesses), has evidently not changed his mind about the value for business of what I call craftsmanship.[85] In *Liberation Management*, he touts the German mittelstand (midsized) companies. His research on these firms led to a PBS show (in May, 1992) on "Germany's quality obsession."[86] I have seen this show and it is one of the clearest examples of the craftsmanship ethic I know. Peters says, "The product is the raison d'etre, the breath of life, for the stellar mittelstanders we visited."[87] For example, he speaks of the success of Playmobil whose owner, Horst Brandstater, concentrates "on product excellence." One of the people to whom the book is dedicated is Hans Beck, the toymaker who "took his apprenticeship as a carpenter, then spent years restoring old furniture."[88] The philosophy of the firm is, itself, central to the notion of craftsmanship. "'This is a toy the child can apply his fantasy to, can change at every moment,' Hans Beck told me. 'He can create new ideas, new stories, new interactions.'"[89]

We have seen that a number of writers on business leadership have emphasized the importance of developing people's latent abilities and inspiring a love of work and a desire to create and achieve—these motives being directed to the goal of quality or excellence. I would suggest that for these writers, the craftsmanship model captures an essential part of a quixotified Sancho Panza vision for business. Such a model, we shall see, has important ethical implications. That any such vision, as a business leader's vision, should have strong ethical implications is reinforced by many writers on business leadership. We have seen that Bennis believes that true leaders are ethical. Nanus thinks that the quixotic vision must be a moral one.[90] Badaracco and Ellsworth, in their interviews with CEOs, asked, "What personal values are more likely to lead to outstanding managerial performance"?[91] First on their list are honesty and fairness (justice) which ground trust and loyalty.[92]

It is necessary to elaborate on our craftsmanship model of managerial statesmanship in order to see how it can help to undermine the moral criticisms of corporate business presented in the previous section. The moral benefits of the craftsmanship model are related, in part, to the basically nonmaterialistic motivation of the craftsman. The advantages of being immoral, e.g., stealing, cheating, and lying, are obvious to a person whose goal in life is narrowly materialistic. Clearly, immorality pays, from a materialistic view, if we can get away with it. However, it is clear that immorality is not advantageous to a lover of craftsmanship. Immorality diminishes, rather than enhances, craftsmanship and therefore would detract from the craftsman's source of happiness. That is, immorality, insofar as it is materialistically oriented, distracts us from the goal of quality and diminishes the satisfaction, dignity, and sense of pride we derive from it. Indeed, Maccoby's experience with craftsmen confirms the fact that they are scrupulously honest and that they essentially respect other people.

If the craftsmanship model can meet Maccoby's and other's requirements concerning just conduct in an organization, can it meet their other requirements? I think that the answer to this question is yes.

When Maccoby analyzes the reasons for the underdeveloped heart, to which he attributes immorality in formal organizations, he mentions a lack of independence, a "hardening" of the heart by a love of power, and careerism (which shields one from the moral impulses that one believes will jeopardize one's career). Craftsmen are models of self-reliant individualists whose self-worth is based upon self-development. The competitiveness of true craftsmen is not directed toward winning in a zero-sum game. Their competitiveness benefits society as well as themselves by the quality of the things (in business, goods and services) that are produced. A craftsman can, indeed, be very competitive, but he or she does not compete by knocking others down. Craftsmen's competitiveness is directed toward achieving some standard of excellence. A craftsmanship ethic is essentially principled and nonmanipulative—it is not winning at all costs but creating something of value that counts. The craftsman's emphasis on quality as the primary goal should shield him from the type of self-manipulation that, according to Maccoby, characterizes careerists.

Finally, We have seen that a quixotified Sancho Panza will not survive well in a business environment that overemphasizes economic values and is heavily bureaucratic. Businesspeople who follow the craftsmanship ideal, however, will be neither overly bureaucratic nor excessively bottom line oriented. Therefore, the adoption of a craftsmanship ethic in business should facilitate the acceptance of a quixotified Sancho Panza.

It will probably be argued that our model is inadequate, for essentially moral qualities of the heart (such as compassion and benevolence), which undermine narrow self-interest or selfishness and direct our attention to others are not consequences of the craftsmanship model. I think this view is too simplistic. The motivations involved in the craftsmanship model are a type of self-interest, but when self-interest is related to self-development, it should not be viewed as opposed to other people's interests. Obviously, a concern for excellence benefits society by providing, in the case of business, quality goods and services, not to mention quality management. But the connection between this sort of self-interest and other people's interest is psychologically and ethically deeper than one might suspect. On the craftsmanship model of self-interest, there is no clear demarcation between acting on self-interest and acting from a concern for others; that is, here, the opposition between self-interest and altruism is nonexistent or, at least, blurred. This type of self-interest relates to a concern for human dignity and worth—values at the heart of *Don Quixote*. The concern for our own worth and dignity extends, especially with proper nurturing, to a concern for human dignity generally. Therefore, an ethic can be developed which prohibits human manipulation and, more positively, helps to nurture respect and concern for people's potentialities. Maccoby's experience with craftsman types confirms this. Since craftsmanship, as I use the term, is a way of expressing what one thinks are the better parts of oneself, what gives one pride and dignity, giving to others has a natural quality. Giving is an expression of oneself, one's accomplishments, in the world. Thus, for example, the dedicated teacher gives of himself or herself from a love of learning. Generally, the craftsman wants to present his work as an expression of the best of himself or herself.

Notes

1.   Thomas J. Donaldson and R. Edward Freeman, *Business as a Humanity* (New York: Oxford University Press, 1994), p. 4.

2.   Richard T. De George, *"Business as a Humanity: A Contradiction in Terms?"* in Thomas J. Donaldson and R. Edward Freeman, *Business as a Humanity* (New York: Oxford University Press, 1994), p. 16.

3.   The term "practice" is intimately related to the term "practical." It connotes what is learned from experience (often repeated)—e.g., skills or expertise—or from action rather than from abstract theory or speculation.

4.   The chivalric hero has been discussed in business ethics. James E. Chesher, for example, contrasts what he calls "the knight in shining armor and the man in the grey flannel suit." He says, "The knight seeks to better the condition of others in the world, the entrepreneur seeks to better his own lot; the knight risks life and limb for the greater good of others, the entrepreneur risks capital (often not his own) for greater personal wealth. The knight has heart and mind turned toward the highest light, the entrepreneur is single-mindedly calculating his own advantage. In short, the knight seems to be standing on high moral ground, and everything he represents, from intention to consequence, seems opposed to the ideals of the entrepreneur" [James E. Chesher, "Business: Myth and Morality," in *Business Ethics and Common Sense*, ed. Robert W. McGee (Westport: Quorum Books, 1992), p. 48].

5.   *The Portable Cervantes*, trans. and ed. by Samuel Putnam (New York: The Viking Press, 1951), p. 202.

6.   Putnam. p. 297.

7.   Irving Kristol, *Neo-Conservatism: The Autobiography of an Idea* (New York: The Free Press, 1995), pp. 184–199.

8.   Kristol, p. 184.

9.   Kristol, p. 184.

10.   Kristol, p. 184.

11.   Kristol, p. 188.

12.   Indeed, some people considered to be intellectuals have preferred, in certain areas, the common sense of the "ordinary" person to the so-called wisdom of certain intellectuals—usually academics. Kristol, who is considered an intellectual, seems to agree with this view. He says, "But even today, the masses of people tend to be

more 'reasonable,' as I would put it, in their political judgment and political expectations than are our intellectuals. The trouble is that our society is breeding more and more 'intellectuals' and fewer common men and women" (Kristol, p. 168).

13. In the introduction to *Don Quixote de la Mancha* [trans. Charles Jarvis (Oxford: Oxford University Press, 1992)], E. C. Riley suggests that the reader perceives the dignity of Don Quixote in spite of the ridicule heaped upon him. Referring to Book II of *Don Quixote*, he says, "Don Quixote, the would-be hero, is now received in mockery as a celebrity, yet he somehow manages to transcend the absurdity of his circumstances by preserving an essential dignity which raises him above the level of the jokers and hoaxers who go to such lengths to get a laugh out of him" (p. xiii).

14. Don Quixote says, "How is it possible for you to have accompanied me all this time without coming to perceive that all the things that have to do with knights-errant appear to be mad, foolish, and chimerical.... Not that they are so in reality; it is simply that there are always a lot of enchanters going about among us, changing things and giving them a deceitful appearance.... So, this that appears to you as a barber's basin is for me Mambrino's helmet, and something else to another person" (Putnam, pp. 262–263). These deceivers, he suggests, deceive others, but not our hero, about the true worth of Mambrino's helmet.

    Don Quixote is called mad because he is thought to be an incurable dreamer. But is it so easy to distinguish dreams from reality? Peter F. Drucker suggests that when President Jimmy Carter "made establishment of Human Rights a goal of American policy and prerequisite to giving American aid," he was ridiculed as a dreamer. "Viewed twenty years later," Drucker says, "he may have been the realist and the dreamers are the believers in the efficacy of the Free Market" [*Managing in A Time of Great Change* (New York: Dutton, 1995), p. 336]. [Drucker argues that "the Free Market will not produce a functioning and growing economy unless it is embedded in a functioning civil society, with effective Human Rights a minimum requirement" (Drucker, p. 337).]

15. Plato is famous for popularizing the view that people are readily deceived by appearances. See, especially, the Allegory of the Cave in the *Republic*.

16. Benedetto Croce, "The '*Simpatia*' of Don Quixote," in *Cervantes Across the Centuries*, eds. Angel Flores and M. J. Benardete (New York: Gordian Press, 1969), p. 189.

17. Croce, p. 190.

18. Croce, p. 191. In Chapter 47 of *Don Quixote*, Cervantes provides clues to his views on fiction which support Croce's interpretation. Fiction should be written so that the impossible is made to appear possible. What is difficult to believe should be entertained and be made entertaining. Therefore, the belief in narrow empiricism,

which relies upon sense experience alone, should be suspended.

19.	Putnam, p. 422.

20.	Putnam, p. 543.

21.	Putnam, p. 536.

22.	Putnam, p. 539.

23.	Putnam, p. 371.

24.	Putnam, p. 523.

25.	Putnam, p. 477.

26.	There is a quixotic element in the *Republic's* (Plato's) view of the wisdom of the philosopher as opposed to the "illusions" of the experienced person. A philosopher who takes this position in the *Republic* seriously and who wishes to practice business ethics will probably have as much trouble convincing businesspeople of his or her wisdom (as opposed to the "illusions" of businesspeople) as Don Quixote has difficulty convincing people that he sees the truth while they see only appearances.

   It seems that Plato is aware of the effect Socrates has on many of the powerful people in Athens, for Socrates was accused, tried, and convicted of corrupting the youth. Indeed, in the *Republic*, when Socrates says that philosophers should be kings, Glaucon, who is very bright but also attracted to worldly values, says, "After hurling at us such an utterance and statement as that, you must expect to be attacked by a great multitude of our men of light and leading, who forthwith will, so to speak, cast off their garments and strip and, snatching the first weapon that comes to hand, rush at you with might and main, prepared to do dreadful deeds" (*Republic* 473e–474a).

   Plato may want the reader to consider the possibility that the potentially effective philosopher king is Glaucon whom Socrates spends the entire *Republic* training. Glaucon, especially as trained by Socrates, is a mean between the extremes of Socrates and the people. Like the famous Alcibiades whom Socrates attempted to educate, Glaucon is much more effective with the people, but he requires Socrates' wisdom to rule well. There is a clear parallel with what I have said about Don Quixote, Sancho Panza, and their relationship. But one difference between Plato and Cervantes is that Cervantes, as we have seen, views the interaction of Don Quixote and Sancho Panza as one of mutual influence for the betterment of both.

27.	The notion of a quixotified Sancho Panza was first mentioned by S. de Madariaga [*'Don Quixote': An Introductory Essay in Psychology* (Westport: Greenwood Press, reprinted 1980)]. This notion is also referred to in more recent discussions of *Don Quixote*. For example, A. J. Close [*Miguel De Cervantes, Don Quixote* (Cambridge:

Cambridge University Press, 1990)] says, "Yet the relative moral stature that he [Sancho] will later assume derives not only from Teresa's brand of self-interested caution ..., but also from Don Quixote's superior wisdom, particularly the second precept of his counsels of government: 'Know thyself'.... Sancho's performance in office is obviously in some sense a fulfillment of those counsels. And his reiterated preference of the soul's welfare to the corrupting effects of climbing the greasy pole ... accords with a dominant, and eventually the prevailing, preoccupation of his master in Part II. So Quixotification is an important factor in Sancho's development ..." (pp. 75–76).

28. William H. Whyte, Jr., *The Organization Man* (New York: Simon and Schuster, 1956).

29. Michael Maccoby, *The Gamesman: The New Corporate Leaders* (New York: Simon and Schuster, 1976), p. 175.

30. Maccoby, p. 178.

31. Maccoby, p. 193.

32. Maccoby, p. 195.

33. William G. Scott and David K. Hart, *Organizational America* (Boston: Houghton Mifflin Co., 1979), p. 27.

34. Joseph L. Badaracco, Jr. and Allen P. Webb ["Business Ethics: A View from the Trenches," *California Management Review* (Winter, 1995): 8–28] interviewed recent graduates of the Harvard MBA Program about their ethical experiences as young managers. The majority of these managers believe that in the large bureaucracies in which they work the senior executives are out of touch with "the real minds of the business" (p. 16) and thus do not exert much ethical influence; top managers, they· maintain, are insulated from the daily functioning of their firms by layers upon layers of bureaucracy.

35. Roger M. D'Aprix, *In Search of a Corporate Soul* (New York: Amacom, 1976), p. 45.

36. Robert Jackall, *Moral Mazes: The World of Corporate Managers* (New York: Oxford University Press, 1988), p. 68.

37. Jackall, p. 124.

38. "Social insulation permits and encourages a lofty viewpoint that, on its face, 'respects the dignity of workers,' but seems devoid of the feel of the texture of workers' lives and of the gut-level empathy that such knowledge can bring"

(Jackall, p. 126).

39. Jackall, p. 46.

40. For the classical position, see, for example, Milton Friedman, "The Social Responsi-bility of Business is to Increase Profits," *New York Times Magazine*, Sept. 13, 1970. (This article has been reprinted in a number of business ethics anthologies.)

41. Leonard Silk and David Vogel, *Ethics and Profits: The Crisis of Confidence in American Business* (New York: Simon and Schuster, 1976), p. 137.

42. Silk and Vogel, p. 209; cf. pp. 112, 233.

43. Irving Kristol, *Two Cheers for Capitalism* (New York: Mentor Book, 1978).

44. George C. Lodge, "The Connection between Ethics and Ideology," *Journal of Business Ethics* (1982): 85–98.

45. E. F. Schumacher, *Small is Beautiful: Economics as if People Mattered* (New York: Perennial Library, 1973), p. 45.

46. S. Prakash Sethi, "Moving from a Socially Responsible to a Socially Accountable Corporation," in *Is The Good Corporation Dead? Social Responsibility in a Global Economy*, eds. John W. Houck and Oliver F. Williams (Boston: Rowman and Littlefield Pubs., 1996), pp. 83–84.

47. Sethi, p. 86.

48. John A. Byrne, *Business Week* (May 9, 1994): 61.

49. Similarly, Gary Hamel and C. K. Prahalad [*Competing for the Future* (Boston: Harvard Business School Press, 1994)] suggest, "One of the inevitable results of downsizing is plummeting employee morale. Employees have a hard time squaring all the talk about the importance of human capital with seemingly indiscriminate cutting.... What employees hear is that they're the firm's most valuable assets; what they know is that they're the most expendable assets" (p. 10).

50. Byrne, p. 61.

51. Thomas J. Peters and Robert H. Waterman, Jr., *In Search of Excellence: Lessons from America's Best-Run Companies* (New York: Warner Books, 1984), p. 56.

52. Peters and Waterman, p. 76.

53. Peters and Waterman, p. 75.

54. Peters and Waterman, p. 82. In the 1980s, management theories that are value driven and people oriented—and therefore potentially more accepting of a quixotified Sancho Panza—were developed by William Ouchi [*Theory Z: How American Business Can Meet The Japanese Challenge* (Reading: Addison-Wesley, 1981)], Richard T. Pascale and Anthony G. Athos [*The Art of Japanese Management: Applications for American Executives*(New York: Warner Books, 1981)], as well as Peters and Waterman and others.

55. Peters and Waterman, p. 83; see James MacGregor Burns, *Leadership*(New York: Harper and Row, 1978), p. 20.

56. Burns, p. 4. Edwin P. Hollander and Lynn R. Offerman ["Power and Leadership in Organizations," in *Contemporary Issues in Leadership*, eds. William E. Rosenback and Robert L. Taylor, 3rd edition (Bolder: Westview Press, 1993)] say that "Although the study of leadership has always presumed the existence of followers, their roles were viewed as essentially passive" (p. 69). They suggest that recent discussions of leadership, however, conceive of the leader-follower relationship as one of mutual influence.

57. Peters and Waterman, p. 282.

58. Peters and Waterman, p. 287.

59. Peters and Waterman, p. 288.

60. Peters and Waterman, p. 287.

61. Marshall Saskin and William E. Rosenback ["A New Leadership Paradigm," in *Contemporary Issues in Leadership*, eds. William E. Rosenback and Robert L. Taylor, 3rd edition (Bolder: Westview Press, 1993)] discuss and evaluate the development, in recent years, of Burns's concept of transforming (or what many now call "transformational") leadership. According to Saskin and Rosenback, Bernard M. Bass developed a measuring tool—Multifactor Leadership Questionnaire (MLQ)—for identifying specific categories and types of transformational leadership behavior. Like Bass, James M. Kouzes and Barry Z. Posner constructed a questionnaire (which the authors believe to be better than Bass's)—the Leadership Practices Inventory (LPI)—to measure transformational leadership. The authors, then, discuss Saskin's questionnaire—based on the work of Warren Bennis, whom I shall consider—the Leadership Behavior Questionnaire (LBQ). The authors emphasize the important point that transformational leaders are guided by moral values and their "vision is based on what the organization and followers need, not what the leader wants personally" (p. 97). With the help of transformational leaders, followers "expand and improve on their own vision," and develop necessary leadership characteristics (p. 98). Thus, they believe that transformational leadership cannot be subsumed under, what they call, "the traditional paradigm of transaction exchange" (p. 103).

62. Ronald A. Heifetz, *Leadership Without Easy Answers* (Cambridge: Belknap Press of Harvard University Press, 1994), p. 18.

63. Heifetz, p. 22.

64. Heifetz, pp. 22–23.

65. Bennis says, "The ultimate morality of bureaucracy is the amorality of segmented acts" [Warren Bennis, *Why Leaders Can't Lead: The Unconscious Conspiracy Continues* (San Francisco: Jossey-Bass Pubs., 1989), p. 95].

66. Warren Bennis, *On Becoming A Leader* (Reading: Addison-Wesley Pub., 1989), p. 192. Joseph L. Badaracco, Jr. and Richard R. Ellsworth emphasize "compelling vision," as does Bennis. They also suggest the need for a quixotified Sancho Panza. Ideals run the risk of being irrelevant unless they are "translated into action" [Joseph L. Badaracco, Jr. and Richard R. Ellsworth, *Leadership and the Quest for Integrity* (Boston: Harvard Business School Press, 1989), p. 109].

   In *Why Leaders Can't Lead*, Bennis distinguishes, as others have, between leaders and managers. "Leaders are people who do the right thing; managers are people who do things right" (p. 18). Good managers are good technicians, while "leaders manage attention through a compelling vision that brings others to a place they have not been before" (p. 19). The vision is made compelling by being made vivid and concrete, e.g., by some metaphor(s) or model.

67. Bennis, *Why Leaders Can't Lead*, p. 109.

68. Bennis, *Why Leaders Can't Lead*, p. 110.

69. Noel M. Tichy and Mary Anne Devanna, *The Transformational Leader* (New York: John Wiley and Sons, 1986), p. 138.

70. Tichy and Devanna say, "Vision implies the ability to picture some future state and to be able to describe the state to others so that they begin to share the dream" (p. 138).

71. Burt Nanus, *Visionary Leadership: Creating a Compelling Sense of Direction for Your Corporation* (San Francisco: Jossey Boss Pubs., 1992), p. 10.

72. Nanus, p. 24.

73. Nanus, pp. 28–29.

74. However, John P. Kotter ["What Leaders Really Do," in *Contemporary Issues in Leadership*, eds. William E. Rosenback and Robert L. Taylor, 3rd edition (Bolder: Westview Press, 1993)] maintains that while managers are supposed to cope with

complexity, leadership, by contrast, deals with change (p. 27). Nonetheless, he too emphasizes the importance for leadership of vision, values, dealing with people's basic needs, courage, and the integrity and trustworthiness of the leader.

75. Bennis, *Why Leaders Can't Lead*, pp. 23–24.

76. Nanus, p. 25.

77. Badaracco and Ellsworth, p. 70.

78. Badaracco and Ellsworth, p. 201.

79. Badaracco and Ellsworth, p. 201.

80. Badaracco and Ellsworth, p. 201.

81. Peters and Waterman blame the so-called rational model of management for denigrating the importance of values, deemphasizing people, and overemphasizing financial analysis. In a statement reminiscent of Maccoby, they say that "the exclusively analytic approach run wild leads to an abstract, heartless philosophy" (Peters and Waterman, p. 45). Although "rational" managers think that they are eminently practical, they are in reality perversely quixotic. They incorporate the "ivory tower" thinking of Don Quixote without his concern for noble or "beautiful" values. Thus, they adopt what is most objectionable in Don Quixote and deemphasize what is most valuable.

82. Rabindra N. Kanungo and Manuel Mendonca [*Ethical Dimensions of Leadership* (Thousand Oaks: Sage Publications, Inc., 1996)], in the context of transformational leadership, consider the question of whether or not leaders have an ethical imperative "to improve their followers for reasons that go well beyond the pragmatic considerations of the 'bottom line'" (p. 70)? They argue, correctly I think, that work is more than a means for earning a living; it is essential to self-development, the development of society, and human dignity. "This vision of the values of human work," they say, "is often blurred, if not gravely distorted, when work is viewed in terms of social exchange theory, as a commodity that is sold by the employee in return for wages and benefits, and the employer, by virtue of his or her ownership of capitol, assumes the right to regard employees as instruments in the production process" (pp. 70–71). They argue that transformational leadership entails an ethical value that does not exist for transactional leadership.

83. My view of a quixotified Sancho Panza as business leader and its connection with a craftsmanship model has certain similarities to the position of Robert Greenleaf [*Servant Leadership: A Journey into the Nature of Legitimate Power and Greatness* (New York: Paulist Press, 1977)]. Greenleaf says, "The servant-leader *is* servant first [a natural servant].... It [servant leadership] begins with the natural feeling that one wants to serve, to serve *first*" (p. 13). He tells us that this position is opposed

to starting with a leader first view (one whose primary drives are often power and wealth). People who are servants first are empathetic and therefore are particularly sensitive to people's needs; they will persevere more than people who are leaders first in developing the best way of fulfilling other's needs. Moreover, a natural servant automatically listens first. My position is similar in that we start with Sancho first to create a Sancho-leader. But a quixotified Sancho Panza is not quite the type of servant that Greenleaf has in mind—he is more worldly and realistic. Which is preferable? I think that businesspeople, in the main, agree with Cervantes's picture of the world. It would seem, then, that we require a Sancho-type servant to deal with it. But Sancho must be transformed by Don Quixote. Sancho does not become squire for noble reasons—he desires wealth, power, and adventure and is somewhat roguish. Yet, he transcends these goals (while understanding them) by gaining admiration for Don Quixote; thus, he learns to be more idealistic and wise. I think that the complexity and the combination of idealism and common sense realism of a Cervantian servant-leader fits better with business than does the more spiritualized version Greenleaf presents. Greenleaf's servant-leader, however, is certainly admirable.

For our purposes, it is also important to mention the connection Greenleaf makes between servant leadership and what he calls a new business ethic. He suggests that a business should exist "as much to provide meaningful work to a person as it exists to provide a product or service to the customer" (p. 142). Business leaders should focus on developing unrealized potential and the satisfaction derived from personal achievement. This business ethic relates servant leadership and a "striving for excellence" as my view connects a quixotified Sancho Panza and a craftsmanship ethic, i.e., the craftsmanship ideal should be at the core of the businessperson's (as servant-leader) vision. [My view of a craftsmanship ethic is developed in Chapter 6 of my book, *Business Ethics: Reflections from a Platonic Point of View* (N.Y.: Peter Lang Publishing, Inc., 1993; reprinted in 1995.)]

84. A good example of such a managerial statesman is Thomas Watson of IBM. Like any good statesman, he thought about the basic values that should guide his organization and emphasized those which truly have intrinsic worth. Above all, having concern for his workers, he encouraged them to develop their abilities; this, he believed, would help them to enjoy and take pride in their work. It would also help them to take pride in the firm. Thus the interests of the workers would coincide with those of the firm. Quality products and services are, of course, the keynotes of such a company.

85. Moreover, in *Liberation Management* [*Liberation Management: Necessary Disorganization for the Nanosecond Nineties* (New York: Alfred A. Knopf, 1992)], he ends his Preface on a quixotic note. "I've allowed myself the unalloyed pleasure of enjoying the mess of market economics powered by lunatics and dreamers, by failure more than success" (p. xxxiv).

86. Peters, *Liberation Management*, p. 529.

87. Peters, *Liberation Management*, p. 550.

88. Peters, *Liberation Management*, p. 532.

89. Peters, *Liberation Management*, p. 532. He also discusses other mittelstand companies such as Trumpf Industries. Again, the emphasis is on product excellence. In an interesting discussion, Peters talks about the balance between theoretical knowledge and practical workmanship, which characterizes the German apprenticeship system. Constantly working with the necessary materials (to understand how best to work with them) is as important as the theoretical ideas; it is "the backbone of Germany's ability to build quality products" (p. 544).

   In his *The Pursuit of Wow* [Tom Peters, *The Pursuit of Wow: Every Person's Guide to Topsy-Turvy Times* (New York: Random House, Vintage, Books, 1994)], he begins by saying, "As of this second, quit doing less-than-excellent work" (p. 1). He suggests that excellence is not everything, but it is basic. Nonetheless, when he discusses ethics (pp. 86–87), he does not connect it with the pursuit of excellence or quality.

90. He says, "Effective leadership empowers an organization to maximize its contribution to the well-being of its members and the larger society of which it is a part" (Nanus, p. 10).

91. Badaracco and Ellsworth, p. 99.

92. "They [the CEOs] believed that the widely accepted conflict between high ethical values and economic performance was, in the long term, a false dichotomy" (Badaracco and Ellsworth, p. 100).

CHAPTER III

Aristotelian Reflections on Theory and Practice in Business Ethics

Introduction

In the previous chapter, I presented arguments for what I call a quixotified Sancho Panza—a model for ethical managerial leadership, which I argued is a *type of* Platonic philosopher king. Such an ideal, I suggested, provides a balance between the extremes of rootless idealistic theory and narrow-minded practicality. It would be unwise to either dismiss or overemphasize theory; rather, one should investigate whether or not a theory is applicable to practice and if it is, the degree to which it is applicable. In this chapter, with the aid of Aristotle, I continue my reflections on how to properly balance theory and practice when dealing with issues in business ethics. I shall argue that an Aristotelian practical philosophy, as applied to business ethics issues, keeps theory and practice in proper balance.[1] I attempt to show this in two parts. In Section 2 (part 1), I suggest that Aristotle's balanced view of the relation between theory and practice in political philosophy can be applied to corporate life; Aristotle's sophisticated ethical and political inquiries should help advocates of corporate culture to construct theories that are theoretically, practically, and ethically sound. Since a corporate culture manifests a corporation's morality or lack of it, corporate culture is of central importance to an ethical corporate leader. In Section 3 (part 2), I argue that theory and practice are kept in proper balance in Aristotle's discussion of *phronēsis* or practical wisdom; this discussion, then, is clearly relevant to the practical wisdom of business leaders and therefore to ethical business leadership. From the standpoint of a proper balance between theory and practice, I suggest, in both parts one and two of this chapter, that an Aristotelian approach to business ethics is preferable to the position of a number of business ethicists who rely on modern ethical theory; I believe they overemphasize theory in business ethics.

It might be helpful, at this point, to elaborate on the subject of ethical theory in business ethics. There is a consensus, at least among philosophers who do business ethics, that some knowledge of ethical theory is necessary in order to deal intelligently with moral problems in corporate business. Contemporary moral theorists who write on business ethics often rely upon a division of normative ethics into teleological and deontological.[2] The primary question for these contemporary moral philosophers is: What is the right thing to do in a particular moral situation? Therefore, their object is actions rather than agents. To answer this question, a rule that fits the situation must be produced and applied. Since we are looking for moral rules to apply to particular situations which are morally problematic, the basic principle(s) appealed to must generate rules to be applied directly to problematic moral situations. Utilitarianism is the most common teleological moral theory; utilitarianism emphasizes the concept of good, and what is right, according to classical utilitarians, is that which is productive of the greatest good for the greatest number. The deontologist, on the contrary, believes that right (or duty), rather than good, is the fundamental moral concept. That which is right ought to be done simply because it is the right thing to do or is our duty. Immanuel Kant is the most famous deontologist. In either case, virtue is handmaiden to another (central) moral concept; that is, in the former case, it is a disposition to produce the greatest possible good and, in the latter, a disposition to do what is morally right or our moral duty.[3]

What in recent years has been called virtue ethics, however, has a different thrust. Virtue ethics theorists, in the main, take their inspiration from ancient Greek philosophers, especially Aristotle. They attempt to make virtue and vice, and therefore the agent, basic to moral theory rather than the intrinsic rightness of, or morally good consequences of, actions.[4]

William C. Frederick presents a picture of philosophic business ethicists. He suggests that these philosophers are like moral knights on a quest. "It was to seek and lay before the corporate barons a Normative Code, no less than a set of declared moral principles that could chart for these worthies and their firms ethical pathways through the field of temptations they might tread in the workaday world."[5] Although Frederick maintains quite rightly that they have at least shown that there are moral principles that may be used for evaluating business conduct, he also suggests that the way they approach business ethics might be considered "unfair, unbalanced, pragmatically unrealistic, and abstractly ideal in the most impracticable manner."[6] Thus, a philosophic knight may be considered by more than a few businesspeople as a Don Quixote who naively attempts to impose normative standards on business activities and businesspeople's relationships without sufficient knowledge (due to lack of experience) of business realities.

Insofar as this picture is accurate, I think that it applies more to certain business ethicists who emphasize modern moral theory than to the few who use Aristotelian ethics.[7] Frederick's criticism seems to pertain to those business ethicists who emphasize the importance of moral principles and rules at the expense of business experience.

Aristotle on Theory and Practice in Business Ethics—Part I

Aristotelian business ethics exhibits a balanced approach to the problem of the place of theory and practice in business ethics. In developing this, we may note an intimate connection between Aristotelian political theory and the way in which many management theorists view corporations. Moreover, the contemporary emphasis on analyzing business environments in terms of corporate cultures[8] seems to be more in line with an Aristotelian (or a virtue ethics) ethical theory than it is with modern ethical theory. Robert Solomon goes so far as to call corporate culture an Aristotelian metaphor.[9] I now turn to the similarity between the notion of corporate culture and Aristotle's concept of a constitution.

Aristotle not only analyzes types of political societies and governments, he often mentions their constitutions. The reason for this is that, for Aristotle, the city should be identified with its constitution. He says, "A constitution is the organization of offices in a state, and determines what is to be the governing body, and what is the end of each community" (*Politics* 1289a15–17). The end is central to a constitution, for it not only determines the distribution of offices, it is also an expression of a way of life for a community. Aristotle says, "The constitution is in a figure the life of the city" (*Politics* 1295a40–1295b1). Different constitutions mold different characters and involve different ways of life.

The obvious connection between a political society and a corporation is that both have a constitution in the sense of possessing some sort of governing structure. But they also have constitutions in the sense that the communities governed have some explicit or implicit end, and the end determines the way of life for both the political and the corporate community. It would seem, then, that the term "corporate culture" is close in meaning to the Aristotelian term "constitution."

In order to develop an Aristotelian business ethic, it is necessary to begin with this central point, the end determines the way of life for both the political and the corporate community. Books VII and VIII of Aristotle's *Politics* consider the construction of an ideal city. The goal of the city, for Aristotle, is the same as that of the individual—*eudaimonia* or happiness (the human good). *Eudaimonia*, according to Aristotle, consists essentially of virtuous activities. Probably, Aristotle would argue that the place of ethics in political theory is analogous to its place in corporate—or, more broadly, organizational—theory. The corporate constitution must consider the good of the corporate community as a whole and this good is defined correctly in terms of virtue.[10]

Aristotle says that moral virtue, as a state of character, involves choosing a mean or an intermediate position between two vicious extremes (excess and defect) with respect to feelings or passions and actions. The mean cannot be determined mathematically—it is imprecise—and it is relative to individuals [NE (*Nicomachean Ethics*) 1106b36–1107a8]. It is this concept of virtue that forms the basis of Aristotle's ideal city.

If this were all that could be said of an Aristotelian conception of business ethics, we would wonder why his view is an improvement over the position of the philosophic knights who overemphasize theory relative to practice. In order to see why Aristotle's position is more balanced, we should consider his approach to political matters and, by analogy, to business.

But before we do this, I first want to suggest that Aristotle's view is a mean between what Frederick considers two principal approaches to business ethics—that of the previously considered philosophic knight and a position he calls behavioral/organization ethics. The former overemphasizes theory while the latter overemphasizes experience (practice). What Frederick calls behavioral/organization ethics is more a management/social science approach than it is philosophical. Behavioral/organization ethics emphasizes the influence of corporate cultures on businesspeople's behavior. Corporate workplaces develop morally relevant perceptions in employees. Frederick says, "These ethical work climates exist as *perceptions* in the minds of employees and managers, who learn that certain normative behaviors are permitted and encouraged while others are forbidden and perhaps punished."[11] Ethical climates can vary from company to company, from division to division within a company, and even from department to department. Thus a relativity of moral values and moral judgments obtains.[12]

Frederick points out an important difference between behavioral/organizational theorists and philosophical theorists (evidently, modern moral philosophers). The latter—philosophic knights—impose standards from above, while the former derive them from within corporate cultures. One benefit of the behavioral/organizational approach is that it is experiential rather than abstract. In this, these theorists are closer to Aristotle than to modern moral theorists. However, being associated with social science more than with philosophy, these behavioral/organizational theorists, unlike moral philosophers, are less willing to judge which normative schemes are more moral. A more balanced approach would combine philosophers' skills in dealing with normative ethical issues with the more experience-based knowledge of behavioral/organizational theorists. This, I suggest, is the approach that Aristotle would take to the problem of developing moral corporate cultures. An Aristotelian approach to business ethics mediates between business ethicists who overemphasize moral theory and those who place too much stress on the importance of business experience and expertise. Indeed, in the *Politics*, Aristotle often plays the arbiter, looking for a mean between extreme positions.

Aristotle evidently considers the empirical study of governments important to political philosophy; it is said that he studied 158 Greek constitutions.[13] Therefore, given our concerns, he would evidently consider the studies of organizational theorists helpful. If, as some Aristotelian commentators suggest, Aristotle collected these *Polities* in order to reform as well as to analyze their constitutions, he certainly would not be satisfied with descriptive and explanatory analyses of these constitutions. In order to see how Aristotle combines the functions of philosophic knights and organizational theorists, it is necessary to show how an Aristotelian statesman functions like a gymnastics teacher or, as he sometimes suggests, a political physician[14].

Aristotle suggests that the art of gymnastics is not merely concerned with what is absolutely best (for that would only suit a nature that is best), but also with what types of training are suitable for the great majority of people, and with what is appropriate for different bodies or for people with specific requirements short of what is ideally best. Similarly, politics must not merely be concerned with the absolutely best city (for such a city requires ideal conditions), but also with the type of constitution that is most desirable for most cities. An ideal constitution would be as impractical for most cities as a rigorous athletic program would be for most people. Aristotle also notes that a proposed form of government should not only be "possible," it should also be "easily attainable by all" (*Politics* 1288b38–39). Moreover, just as gymnastics should consider what is necessary for different bodies which require training short of what is ideally best, so the statesman must know what is best for each kind of body politic, e.g., for "inferior" cities for which an ideally best, or even a practically best, model is unsuitable. Therefore, where Aristotle's second best city is impractical, the statesman must find other alternatives which can be applied to the peculiar circumstances and difficulties of these cities so as to improve them as much as possible.[15]

Just as the statesman must study all varieties of government as well as an ideal form of government—in order to "find remedies for the defects of existing constitutions" (*Politics* 1289a7)—so the philosopher of corporate culture must not only attempt to determine some ideal type of corporate culture (from a moral point of view), he or she should study existing corporate cultures in order to determine what remedies are necessary to make them as morally acceptable as possible.[16]

It might be helpful, at this point, to summarize what an Aristotelian approach to corporate culture might be. Aristotle believes that it is necessary to approach politics with a well-developed, correct ethical theory—one which properly defines the human good or happiness (*eudaimonia*). This leads to Aristotle's virtue ethics, which guides his discussion of politics from the most ideal to increasingly perverse forms of government.[17] However, he also believes that it is essential to engage in the historical and descriptive project of determining the number and nature of extant constitutions, for analyses of these constitutions provide the material which enables us to formulate the best practicable city and provide cures, which have ethical significance, for "inferior" types of cities such as those with democratic and oligarchic regimes. An Aristotelian business ethics, then, must be based upon a correct view of the human good and consequently a defensible virtue ethic. But this endeavor must be balanced by a careful and thorough analysis of existing corporations, emphasizing their corporate cultures. One should determine the number and types of these corporate cultures, their differences, and the various ways in which they can be combined, for this analysis will provide the material which the business ethics theorist must use to develop ethically viable and practical corporate cultures. Thus, besides determining what an ideal corporate culture (in an Aristotelian sense) might be—by applying the Aristotelian mean (moral virtue) to ideal circumstances and conditions—the business ethics theorist must also develop, from the material he or she has gathered, the best corporate culture from a practical standpoint; to use Aristotle's language, a corporate culture should be developed which is the most desirable for most corporations, i.e., one which is both practically possible and easily attainable by all. Such a corporate culture would incorporate as much of Aristotle's ideal of moral virtue as possible (and, therefore, as much *eudaimonia* as possible) for the greatest number of its members. Finally, by discovering the most dominant types of corporate cultures—paralleling Aristotle's search for the most dominant types of constitutions—the business ethics theorist, armed with a knowledge of moral virtue, can provide the proper medicine to help "inferior" corporate cultures to both survive and be as ethically viable as possible.

It may be helpful to illustrate how Aristotelian "medicine" might be applied to existing corporate cultures. I shall first consider how oligarchic business practices can be moderated—and thus be made more virtuous—by injecting into oligarchic business cultures a healthy dose of what Aristotle would call the aristocratic ideal (a concern for excellence).

The position of the oligarch has been traditionally the dominant view of business; it is expressed in what has been called the classical creed of business—business has no social responsibilities other than to produce goods and services efficiently, make money for shareholders, and conduct business in a lawful manner.[18] According to Thomas J. Peters and Robert H. Waterman, Jr. firms that emphasize quality and reliable products and services and concern for people, i.e., corporations that stress "excellence" (the original meaning of "virtue"), do better than oligarchic firms which overemphasize finance and quantitative analysis.[19] To use Aristotelian language, oligarchic firms must be taught moderation and, generally, the value of virtue, i.e, the "medicine" of the Aristotelian mean should be applied to such firms. In the previous chapter, we said that Peters and Waterman maintain that the values of "excellent" corporations create a more moral atmosphere than do bottom line dominated firms and promise dignity to employees—a quality central to Aristotelian virtue. We saw that they suggest that "excellent" firms create environments in which employees can develop their abilities and be treated with respect and dignity. I suggested that "excellent" firms embody the craftsmanship ethic—the goal of craftsmanship is to create that which has quality or excellence; motivations for craftsmen include personal satisfaction, pride in accomplishment, and a sense of dignity derived from a concern for self-development. The inclusion of a healthy dose of the craftsmanship ideal in an oligarchic corporation will moderate its tendency to overemphasize the importance of the bottom line, and the acceptance of this more moderate position—one which stresses the importance of both profit (the oligarchic view) and excellence (the craftsmanship ideal)—tends, then, towards a mean position. An Aristotelian would maintain that the resulting corporate culture would produce more moral virtue and happiness than would the original oligarchic culture.

Since an Aristotelian business ethic should include an analysis of historical, e.g., American, corporate cultures, it is important to show how morally deficient character types that have been molded by these cultures can be modified so they can be brought more in line with the Aristotelian ethical model. I shall provide an illustration of how this might be done.

If we examine American business character models, e.g., those mentioned by Michael Maccoby in the *Gamesman*, we may see how the importance of the mean naturally arises from a consideration of how to modify the inadequacies of such models. Many businesspeople believe that the growth of business in the 1970s depended upon the modification of the organization (or company) man's managerial style by that of traditional American business individualism.[20] The gamesman seems to be the result.

The character of the organization man, apparently, is not entrepreneurial enough to meet the challenges of rapid change, and organizational stagnation is the result. In attempting to compensate for the deficiencies of the organization man, there is a natural tendency to appeal, at least unconsciously, to counterbalancing traits found in a more traditional American business character model—the traits of the historic entrepreneur illustrated by the robber barons of the late 1800s and early 1900s. This, it would seem, is what happened in American management in the 1970s.

According to Michael Maccoby, the gamesman character model dominated the upper echelons of management in the 1970s. This model appears to be a combination of the jungle fighter (the prototype is the robber baron) and the organization man (Maccoby's company man). For the jungle fighter, winning is the basic goal, and this is achieved by being tough, aggressive, taking calculated risks, exhibiting great energy, innovativeness, being unafraid of change, priding oneself on one's individuality, being contemptuous of weakness, and the like. In Maccoby's gamesman, these qualities are combined with those of the organization man. Gamesmen are team players; they are also cooperative, dependent on the game and others in the organization, and they derive basic meaning in life from the organizational games played. The gamesman as a mean between more extreme character types—the jungle fighter and organization man—displays some positive moral character traits not possessed by jungle fighters and some that the organization man does not have. Thus, Maccoby shows, for example, that, unlike the jungle fighter, the gamesman is unprejudiced or fair, not destructive, does not relish defeating others, and is not nasty or vindictive, while he or she demonstrates courage, initiative, and other positive traits that are not part of the organization man's character. However, some of the moral inadequacies of this character type are also predictable. Like the jungle fighter or robber baron, the gamesman is basically unfeeling, unprincipled, and manipulative. He or she is not compassionate and generally is not motivated by issues related to social responsibility. The gamesman, therefore, is not a proper ethical model for business leadership. Although he or she is morally preferable to the jungle fighter or robber baron, this model is not adequate for a best practicable business organization,[21] i.e., it is not an adequate mean.

Peters and Waterman provide an interesting example of how to use what I have called the craftsmanship ideal to properly mix concerns of the organization man and the traditional entrepreneur. Stability is necessary with respect to basic values; there should be an emphasis on excellent products and service (love of product, quality, production through people) and a value system that supports and implements them. Entrepreneurial attitudes and habit breaking are necessary because of business's need for the avoidance of stagnation through regular innovation. The desire for stability and security (basic concerns of the organization man) is mixed with entrepreneurial and habit breaking attitudes, according to these management theorists, by excellent companies emphasizing so-called loose-tight properties. These companies are most rigid (tight) about their basic values (evidently, quality and reliable products and service and concern for people), and they demand and get conformity with regard to these values. The cultures of excellent companies, in this way, cater to organization man values; they cater to our security and stability needs and provide their members with a sense of belongingness or meaning (purpose). The excessive conformity and willingness to give up authority, which traditionally are concomitant with the above attitudes, are compensated for in excellent companies by an emphasis on creating environments in which employees can develop their abilities and on what Peters and Waterman call autonomy—the basis of the loose properties. The shared values provide a sense of purpose and stability, while the firms also encourage autonomy by allowing more experimentation and some failures.

Let us consider further how the craftsmanship ideal can be used to moderate the extreme tendencies of organization man and robber baron values. Peters and Waterman maintain that shared values provide businesspeople with a sense of place, security, and stability. A sense of belongingness (meaning and purpose in their lives) is derived from the specified higher, more "beautiful" values. Since traditionally, in the history of American business values, such values are associated with organization men, it is helpful to show that the craftsmanship ideal can control the development of extreme organization man traits and their consequent inadequate moral and organizational effects.

Organization men exhibit traits of excessively temperate people; in their extreme form, as suggested in Chapter 2, Section 4, they are submissive conformists who depend upon authority, and they sacrifice courage and integrity for security (stability) and comfort. Craftsmen, however, are models of self-reliant individualists whose self-worth is based upon self-development. No wonder Peters and Waterman talk about autonomy as counterbalancing a willingness to conform and give up authority. Craftsmen are noted for their integrity, and instead of being motivated by fear (the stick), which nurtures cowardice, their conduct is guided by a concern for quality. Moreover, an excessive concern for security, comfort, and material goods are not basic values for the craftsman. Their complaint is often that the world is too materialistic, too concerned with comfort and security.

We also saw that organization men are bureaucrats—they stick to the rules—and in their extreme form, they reduce morality to a superficial concern for manners. This is, in part, due to a softness in character, an excessive concern for peace and order. An emphasis on excellence or quality, however, breeds the opposite of superficiality. Since a craftsmanship value system is based upon creating that which is substantive, rather than the appearance or image of that which is substantive, substantial rather than superficial human relations are emphasized. Finally, since craftsmen are not bureaucrats, their sense of autonomy will moderate the negative effects of bureaucratic tendencies in an organization.

Among modern managers, especially in the upper echelons of

corporate business, there is still admiration for the traditional individ-
ualistic American business character model—that of the traditional
entrepreneur. Moreover, we have seen that, according to Maccoby, many
modern upper echelon managers are gamesmen. Can the craftsmanship
ideal perform the same function with these models that it does with the
organization man model? I think it can. I shall first show that the
craftsmanship ideal can moderate excessively courageous traits associated
with the traditional American entrepreneur.

The selfishness associated with what might be called the robber
baron form of individualism will tend to be moderated by the craftsmanship ideal. The excessive desire to win at all costs, using extremely
competitive means, has tended to mold a hard, cold, unprincipled, and
manipulative business character. We saw that the gamesman, whom
Maccoby thinks is a moral improvement on the jungle fighter, exhibits,
to some extent, the above negative moral traits. Winning, on this view,
seems to take place within a zero-sum game. But we have seen that the
competitiveness of craftsmen is quite different. As previously suggested,
craftsmen can be very competitive, but they do not compete by knocking
others down. Their competitiveness is directed toward achieving some
standard of excellence; they are competitive with themselves. Therefore,
their competitiveness and desire to succeed benefit society as well as
themselves. A craftsmanship ethic is essentially principled and nonmanipulative; creating something of value, not winning at all costs, is what
counts.

Some of the excessively selfish, antisocial effects of robber baron
individualism can be modified by viewing individualism and being a part
of some whole as compatible rather than as essentially in conflict. The
whole should be organized in such a way that business provides its
employees with the opportunity to develop and express their capabilities.
This is the view of Peters and Waterman. This position respects a concern
for individuality while recognizing the organizational needs of modern
business. Insisting upon following outmoded, rather than updated,
definitions of traditional American business concepts such as individualism may be the most dangerous form of business inflexibility.

Aristotle on Theory and Practice in Business Ethics—Part 2

In contrast to Frederick's philosophic knights (as business ethicists), whose approach to business ethics is heavily laden with theory, I have argued that an Aristotelian business ethic would apply Aristotle's concept of virtue to corporations so that neither the experiential or practical aspect of corporate cultures nor the more theory-based reflections on ethics are overemphasized. In this section of the chapter, I shall continue this contrast between philosophic knights and Aristotelian ethicists. I shall attempt to show that the practical wisdom or *phronēsis* that many modern moral philosophers hope to bring to business is too theory laden insofar as it depends heavily upon the application of moral principles and rules, while Aristotelian *phronēsis* exhibits a balance between theory and practice or experience.

In "Ethics and the Craft Analogy," James Wallace suggests that after considering Aristotle's discussion of *phronēsis* or practical wisdom, "one is no wiser about *how* the *phronimos* [the practically wise person] properly determines what choice should be made, what course of action should be undertaken."[22] Wallace thinks that an account of the rules or principles the *phronimos* uses is necessary if virtue ethics is to furnish a guide for determining sound ethical beliefs. He seems to think that *phronēsis* and the virtues themselves are analogous to crafts (*technai*)—rules or principles are required for the proper performance of practical wisdom and the virtues. Is the notion of craft or *technē* sufficient to explicate the idea of *phronēsis*? This question is particularly important because a number of business ethicists who stress modern moral philosophy seem to agree with Wallace.

In the first paragraph of Chapter 8 of the *Nicomachean Ethics*, Aristotle distinguishes between two senses of "practical wisdom"—I shall call them *phronēsis¹* and *phronēsis²*. *Phronēsis¹* is the wisdom derived from political and ethical inquiry. *Phronēsis²* is practical wisdom with respect to particulars or actions (and it relates to deliberation). *Phronēsis¹* is quite different from *phronēsis²* and is theory-laden. Theories about virtues may themselves be more or less specific; we may give an account—with various degrees of specificity—of particular virtues as well as virtue in general. Nonetheless, our inquiry remains at the level of theory and is different from practical wisdom's deliberations about actions and particulars. For Aristotle, the goal of ethics is practical rather than theoretical—we do not pursue ethics primarily for its own sake. However, knowledge of thè virtues, which is based upon *phronēsis[1]* (that which provides theories of virtue and the virtues) is necessary for *phronēsis[2]*.

In distinguishing between *phronēsis* and *technē* in what follows, emphasis is placed on *phronēsis[2]*, for in business ethics, we are concerned with making moral choices and decisions. *Phronēsis[2]*, I shall argue, cannot be properly explicated by the concept of *technē*.

Aristotle contrasts both *phronēsis* and *technē* (considered as practical in a broad sense) with theoretical knowledge (See, for example, NE 1139a27–28, 1178b20–21, *Metaphysics* 1025b25, and *Topics* 145a15–16). *Phronēsis* and *technē* pertain to a realm that is variable and inexact, while theoretical knowledge relates to what is invariable and precise. For Aristotle, however, the practical in its strict sense (*praxis*) is equivalent to *phronēsis*, and *technē* is identified with productive (*poietike*) knowledge. *Technē* involves an activity that makes something which is separate from, and is the goal of, activity; *phronēsis* pertains to the conduct of one's life, the goal being the activity itself. Thus, the craftsman is separate from what he or she creates, but the ethical agent as *phronimos* is clearly not separate from his or her actions. Although Aristotle does suggest that the concept of *technē* or craft is helpful in ethics, his analysis shows that he believes *phronēsis* and *technē* to be different concepts, and that the former notion is central to ethics.

Since Aristotle believes that ethical phenomena are quite diverse and heterogeneous, ethics cannot be subsumed under a specific *technē*. Moreover, the concept of *technē* is closer to theoretical knowledge than is *phronēsis*.[23] Aristotle distinguishes between the technician and the person of experience (*Metaphysics* 981a24–30); the technician strives to gain knowledge of the universal which is applied to experience, while the knowledge of the experienced person, like that of the *phronimos*, is more concrete and particular. Therefore, one reason why Aristotle does not make technical knowledge central to ethics is that much of the *phronimos's* knowledge pertains to particulars, and *technē* provides knowledge of general rules, not particular cases.[24]

We have seen that business ethicists who emphasize modern moral theory rely heavily on moral principles and rules derived from them. These rules are applied to moral problems in business to generate answers to these problems. Such a view treats business ethics as a *technē* and, therefore, is skewed more towards theory than is Aristotelian *phronēsis*; clearly, then, Aristotle would disagree with this position. His view, then, requires elaboration.

For Aristotle, *phronēsis* has an essential ethical component. The Greeks admired resourcefulness, opportunism, and general subtlety of mind in dealing with contingency and chance—with transient, shifting, and ambiguous situations. Homer's "wily" Odysseus is a famous Greek hero. But Aristotelian prudence differs from Machiavellian prudence as moral virtue differs from expediency. In the *phronimos*, Aristotle combines moral virtue and the flexibility and subtlety recognized in such areas as oratory, politics, medicine, and navigation. Although the *phronimos* does not make moral decisions by applying moral rules or principles, his or her excellences of character (moral virtues) are necessary conditions for *phronēsis* and serve as implicit principles for guiding conduct. Thus, the *phronimos* can be said to have knowledge of the virtues as general principles, but they are not applied directly to actions or situations as craftsmen apply the rules or principles of their *technai* to the materials with which they work. In mediating between virtues (as general principles) and particulars, the *phronimos* emphasizes experience, and the perceptiveness and sensitivity that it can provide. In this sense, the *phronimos* is more like the experienced person than the technician. The *phronimos* must be morally virtuous in order to discern ends that are truly good; ethical knowledge proceeds from good character.[25] However, the reverse is also the case; one cannot be morally virtuous without *phronēsis*. This circle is not vicious; that is why Aristotle both acknowledges and accepts it. Moral virtues, as morally good habits, arise from repeated experiences that are good and these experiences help to develop our moral perceptiveness and sensitivity so essential to *phronēsis*. More specifically, the *phronimos's* perception or insight seems to be formed by reflecting on experiences in aiming at the mean (Aristotelian moral virtue). *Phronēsis*, then, being practical wisdom, can guide actions. Thus, it is both a guide to good actions and arises from good actions. *Phronēsis* guides action through knowledge of both general principles (the virtues) and particulars.[26]

An unhelpful model for understanding *phronēsis* is a deductive model, which uses a set of rules which make the minor premises unproblematic, e.g., stealing is wrong; John stole X; therefore, what John did was wrong. *Phronēsis* is necessary where the minor premises are not so obvious. Aristotelian moral virtues are different from general rules. When, for example, the technician applies general rules, the particulars to which the rules are applied are indicated by the rules. We determine the minor premise by seeing whether or not the instance we are considering is an actual instance of the rule. Aristotelian virtues are indeterminate, but *phronēsis* makes the more determinate judgment in each particular case. The moral person is armed with a knowledge of virtue—a knowledge of different means between extremes (excess and defect)—which are indeterminate with reference to particulars; we have seen that the mean cannot be determined mathematically—it is imprecise—and it is relative to individuals. *Phronēsis* makes a correct judgment in particular cases by choosing the right times, occasions, objects, people, motive (choosing virtuous actions for their own sakes), and manner (NE 1106b20–23). The *phronimos's* judgments are based upon perceptions or insights and are not easy to make (NE 1109a24–29). Aristotle says,

> But up to what point and to what extent a man must deviate [from the mean] before he becomes blameworthy it is not easy to determine by reasoning, any more than anything else that is perceived by the senses; such things depend upon particular facts, and the decision rests with perception (NE 1109b19–23).

Since the *phronimos's* wisdom depends so much on experience, one might tend to neglect the importance of the moral virtues. Knowledge of human virtue or right principles of conduct (the human good), however, is essential for, says Aristotle, "like archers who have a mark to aim at," this knowledge provides a goal for guiding conduct (NE 1094a24–25).[27] Thus, like an archer, a morally virtuous person will score a better hit by recognizing the direction in which he or she must look and the things to which she must pay attention. But the *phronimos* is not going to hit what is right by the use of some art (*technē*), by following some rule. Practical wisdom is impossible without moral virtue because the latter provides a disposition to aim at proper human goals and to consider the particularities of a given problem in the light of these goals. Aiming at correct goals—the moral virtues—helps Aristotle to differentiate between practical wisdom and cleverness.

I have attempted to show that Wallace's criticism of Aristotle is based upon the false assumption that there are, as he puts it, standards for determining practical wisdom. Thus, he is unwilling to look to the solution that Aristotle offers—the resourcefulness of both mind and character that is required because there are no such rules or principles for making one practically wise. Aristotle, himself, provides a model for the *phronimos*—in our case, an ethical corporate leader—in his role as a political physician. We have seen that the *phronimos* combines moral virtue (and the knowledge of moral virtue) with the flexibility and subtlety necessary in such arts as medicine, navigation, and gymnastics. Aristotle, as *phronimos*, does not directly apply rules or principles, i.e., the principle of the mean or the specific virtues, to political regimes; rather, what is applied is insight (perceptiveness) which develops from a combination of moral virtue (and understanding principles of virtue) and experience—in this case, experience gained from studying political regimes and in making sound moral judgments.

As in the case of a person's moral virtue, so in the case of corporate moral activity, the correct mean is relative. As Aristotle suggests, the mean is indeterminate with respect to particulars; the *phronimos* must make a more determinate judgment in each particular case. Thus, what is best for an ideal corporation (what is absolutely best) would not suit most firms. The mean must be adapted to different types of people as well as to the peculiar circumstances, conditions, (etc.) of specific corporations so that what is demanded is both attainable and the morally best that is possible under the circumstances.

You may recall that in Section 3, I mentioned two quotations (see notes 11 and 12) pertaining to Frederick's discussion of the behavioral/organizational approach to business ethics. We saw that these business ethicists emphasize the influences of corporate cultures on businesspeople's behavior;[28] specifically, the morality of corporate cultures is absorbed by employees and managers as perceptions. A firm's ethics is said to be sent as "signals" through "perceptual pathways" establishing and reinforcing "ethically acceptable ways of behaving and making workplace decisions."

If the ethical consciousness of a corporate member functions as perceptions derived from the firm's culture, business ethicists should recognize that the corporate *experience* will have considerably more effect on the morality of businesspeople than the application of any set of explicit moral rules taught by philosophic knights. What is essential here is the development of good ethical character traits. Sound ethical perceptions are determined by a combination of moral virtue—which, at best, includes an understanding of its principles—and experience in making sound moral judgments. An Aristotelian corporate culture approach to business ethics, then, entails Aristotle's conception of *phronēsis* as the basis of sound moral judgment. An ethically ideal corporate culture is necessary for the development of a high degree of *phronēsis*. If circumstances and conditions preclude the possibility of such a corporate culture, we saw that we should aim for the development of an ethical corporate culture which is practically possible for most corporations. Such corporate cultures would help to cultivate ethical perceptions which are as sound as is practically possible, given the materials with which a *phronimos* has to work. Finally, even inferior corporate cultures, from a ethical point of view, can be helped by doses of Aristotelian medicine so that the ethical perceptions of members of these firms will be improved as much as the corporate culture will allow.

I have suggested a scale of *technai* from those such as grammar where knowledge of general rules should be emphasized to those such as navigation where such knowledge is not adequate to solve all individual cases.[29] The navigator, then, is more like the *phronimos* than he or she is like the grammarian. An interesting example of this is given by Mark Twain in Chapter 8, "Perplexing Lessons," of *Life on the Mississippi*. Mark Twain reflects on the difficulties of navigating the Mississippi river. He is told by Mr. Bixby that he must know the shape of the river perfectly, for he must navigate it at night. He must learn to distinguish between the shadows cast by "a clear starlight night" and the true shoreline as well as the seeming straight lines of the shore on "a pitch-dark night" and the true shoreline. But on nights when there is a gray mist, the shoreline has no particular shape at all. Moreover, different kinds of moonlight change the shape of the river in different ways. The young Mark Twain is confused: "Have I got to learn the shape of the river according to all these five hundred thousand different ways?" But even if the navigator learns the shape of the river by heart, his or her problems are far from over, for the shore is constantly changing its shape. Mark Twain concludes,

> Two things seemed pretty apparent to me. One was that in order to be a pilot a man had got to learn more than any one man ought to be allowed to know; and the other was, that he must learn it all over again in a different way every twenty four hours. (The above quotations can be found in the first three pages of the chapter.)

But knowing about the shore is not sufficient. One must know the exact spots of shoal water, if one intends to stay afloat; you must be able to identify reefs and distinguish them from apparent reefs (caused by the wind). And when Mark Twain had mastered such knowledge and thought that his education was complete, he was taught by Mr. Bixby that there was much more to learn. Mark Twain could have sought refuge in the belief that Mr. Bixby was wrong. He could have argued that Mr. Bixby learned the river by experience, but there must be rules and principles which are readily applicable that can yield knowledge of the river more easily; that is, we can learn an appropriate *technē* rather than having to rely primarily on experience. Fortunately, Mark Twain did not succumb to this false view in the way in which some moral philosophers have succumbed to the lure of rules and principles at the expense of moral experience.

We have seen that if we are going to draw an analogy between moral theory and *technai* or crafts, modern moral theory, which looks to rules and principles to solve concrete moral problems, would fit the bill better than Aristotelian ethics. In business ethics, consequentialist, e.g., utilitarian, and/or Kantian principles are often used to attempt to solve moral problems in business. I believe that Joel Kupperman is correct when he says that "despite the opposition between Kantians and consequentialists, it is easy for someone who is reading some of the works of either school to get the picture of an essentially faceless ethical agent who is equipped by theory to make moral choices that lack psychological connection with either the agent's past or future."[30] Why not, then, dispense with Aristotelian moral virtue and *phronēsis*? Are moral rules or principles applied in a Kantian or consequentialist way sufficient to solve moral problems? Kupperman says, "It simply is easier, in the general run of cases, to be aware that something would count as stealing or killing than to be aware that something would count as damaging another person's life."[31] Thus, moral sensitivity is necessary to apply, at least, some of the moral rules, and concern is required to take relevant facts seriously. For example, Kupperman suggests that in order to use Kant's categorical imperative, we must formulate rules (maxims) to be tested, and these maxims will be stated in different ways depending upon how different our moral traditions are. Thus, the way maxims are perceived is dependent upon the type of character nurtured in a moral tradition.[32] Concerning consequentialism, it has been argued that it is difficult to know the future consequences of actions. Be this as it may, the consequences that we do consider relate to our moral perceptions of what is relevant. Generally, *phronēsis*—which we have seen is intimately related to good character—is necessary to perceive adequately ethically salient and relevant factors that are involved in ethically problematic situations. Indeed, I should think that *phronēsis* is necessary to perceive certain situations as ethically problematic or even as involving something of ethical significance. It would seem, then, that modern ethical theory, with its emphasis on rules and principles, cannot substitute for Aristotelian *phronēsis*.[33] If Aristotle is correct, then, it is his view rather than that of Frederick's philosophic knights (qua modern moral philosophers) which correctly balances theory and practice in business ethics. Moreover, the objections to philosophic knights as being too theoretical, abstract, and impractical are not relevant to Aristotle's *phronimos*, and, therefore, Aristotle's ethics should be congenial to many businesspeople.

What I have said about modern moral theory is not meant to deny its usefulness; rather, it is meant to show that if a moral agent neglects Aristotelian *phronēsis* (and the emphasis on moral character or virtue), he or she does not have the tools to mediate adequately between moral rules and principles and moral problems.

In contrasting classical and modern ethical theory, it is important to note that the former involves a broader notion of the realm of ethical issues than does the latter. I shall conclude this chapter with a discussion of this point. Classical ethics (that of Socrates, Plato, and Aristotle) raises as its fundamental question: What is the good life for human beings? The question is quite different from the one raised by modern moral philosophers and involves a broader conception of what is ethical. The answer given by the classical view is that the activities based upon human excellences (moral and intellectual) constitute the good life for human beings. Since modern moral philosophy has a narrower conception of ethics than the ancients do, there is a sense in which the former conception of ethics makes fewer demands on the total person than the classical view does. The contrast between modern and classical ethics requires some elaboration.

In the classical conception of ethics, ethics permeates every facet of one's life, for it is concerned with the human good in general. However, modern moral theory often distinguishes between moral considerations and those which pertain to personal ideals. One distinction, then, which must be emphasized if we are to concern ourselves with recognizing certain situations as ethically problematic or as involving something of ethical significance is that between the neat division of situations into moral and nonmoral that many modern moral theorists posit and the lack of such a division in classical moral theory. Questions about friends, whom to marry, careers, and the like are expelled from the moral realm as nonmoral by modern moral philosophy. But on the classical view, these questions, and generally life's major questions, are related to character and, therefore, have ethical significance. It is clear, then, that whether business accepts the modern or the classical model of ethical theory makes a great deal of difference in the way a businessperson will perceive moral problems.

Notes

1. Readers of Aristotle may remember that he distinguishes between two different senses of what may be called economics. He approves of *oecinomicus* (household trading), but he disapproves totally of *chrematisike* (trade for profit). It would seem that Aristotle disapproves of business in the modern sense; how, then, can one take an Aristotelian approach to the problems of business ethics? It may not be surprising, therefore, to find that Denis Collins says that articles on Aristotle and

business theory have not been indexed in the *Business Periodical Index* for the past twenty years ["Aristotle and Business," *Journal of Business Ethics* 6 (1987): 571, n.1]. He attributes this, not unrealistically, to the impression Aristotle gives of being antibusiness and antiprofit (Collins, p. 567). Nonetheless, he argues that if Aristotle were to write today, he would be probusiness and proprofit (Collins, p. 567). Using Aristotelian premises, he speculates about the nature of an Aristotelian business corporation and how profit could be an acceptable goal of business. Even as late as 1993, we find Robert C. Solomon raising the issue of "coupling" Aristotle and business ethics. He says, "It is Aristotle who initiates so much of the history of business ethics as a wholesale attack on business and its practices. Aristotelian prejudices underlie much of business criticism and the contempt for finance that preoccupies so much of Christian ethics" ["Corporate Roles, Personal Virtues, Moral Mazes: An Aristotelian Approach to Business Ethics" in *Business Ethics and the Law*, eds. C. A. J. Coady and C. J. G. Sampford (Sidney: The Federal Press, 1993), p. 30]. However, as his title suggests, Solomon believes—I think correctly—that Aristotle has a great deal to contribute to business ethics. He thinks that business ethics, as I have suggested, should be more concerned with discussions of character or virtue than with the application of abstract principles, e.g., Kantianism and utilitarianism; he maintains that Aristotle has much to contribute in this regard. Solomon develops an Aristotelian "framework of virtue ethics in business" (Solomon, pp. 36–41). In *Ethics and Excellence: Cooperation and Integrity in Business* (New York: Oxford University Press, 1993), he discusses, in detail, what he considers to be an Aristotelian approach to business ethics. Ronald F. Duska agrees, as I do, with Solomon's evaluation of the traditional approach to the solution of business ethics problems. He argues against most business ethics texts which attempt to solve business ethics problems by applying utilitarian and/or deontological principles to "particular actions, general practices or overarching social systems" ["Aristotle: A Pre-Modern Post-Modern? Implications for Business Ethics," *Business Ethics Quarterly* 3 (1993): 232]. He believes that Aristotle's *Rhetoric* provides a method that is most helpful to doing business ethics. He especially emphasizes Aristotle's enthymematic method of relying on agreed upon premises to get others to see things in the way we do (Duska, p. 241). He maintains that the Aristotelian approach is a substitute for an inadequate ethical theory which involves the application of rules. I might mention that Duska's interesting discussion would have benefitted from an analysis of Aristotle's use of dialectic in the *Nicomachean Ethics*. Dialectic employs the type of Aristotelian premises of which he approves—*endoxa* (generally agreed upon opinions). He seems, however, to reject a dialectical approach as useful in applied ethics (Duska, pp. 248–249, n. 44).

Since the late 1980s, there have been other instances of the use of an Aristotelian approach to business ethics. The following are some examples. In "Aristotle and Fair Deals" [*Journal of Business Ethics* 7 (1988): 681–690], Ronald A. Cordero uses Aristotle's account of fair and unfair exchanges and deals to answer the following questions. "When is an exchange a fair exchange? And when is a deal (an agreement to make an exchange) a fair deal" (Cordero, p. 681)? He emphasizes the virtues of liberality and magnificence which, like all Aristotelian virtues, involve choosing a mean between extremes. David Cruise Malloy and

Donald L. Lang, in their article, "An Aristotelian Approach to Case Study Analysis" [*Journal of Business Ethics* 12 (1993): 511–516], develop what they call "an alternative and comprehensive approach to the traditional case study method (quantitative methods that emphasize the bottom line) by incorporating Aristotle's metaphysical analysis of causes" (Malloy and Lang, p. 511)—his famous four causes (material, efficient, formal, and final). Aristotle's model for causality is applied, as a case study, to a problem in a Mazda plant in Michigan. Charles M. Horvath, in his paper "Excellence V. Effectiveness: MacIntyre's Critique of Business" [*Business Ethics Quarterly* 5 (July 1995): 499–532], discusses Alasdair MacIntyre's belief that an Aristotelian system of virtue ethics should be seriously considered by business managers. Albert Anderson applies Aristotle's ethics of character to philanthropy ["Aristotle and the Ethics of Philanthropy" in *The Responsibilities of Wealth*, ed. Dwight F. Burlingame (Bloomington: Indiana University Press, 1992), pp. 51–65]. Steven M. Minz ["Aristotelian Virtue and Business Ethics Education," *Journal of Business Ethics* 15 (August 1996): 827–838] recognizes that there is increased interest in applying Aristotelian ethics to business. He supports the integration of Aristotelian virtue ethics into business curriculums. For related references, the reader should look at note 4.

2. See, for example, Robbin Derry and Ronald M. Green, "Ethical Theory in Business Ethics: a Critical Assessment," *Journal of Business Ethics* (1989): 522–523. The authors survey leading business ethics texts and conclude the following about the texts that include a chapter(s) on ethical theory. "Almost without exception," they say, "these discussions [in the works they examine] begin by categorizing these [ethical] theories under two broad headings: consequentialist (or teleological) and nonconsequentialist (deontological) views" (p. 522). It is interesting to note that there is no mention in the article of the classical tradition of ethics, which emphasizes character or virtue; it is as if this tradition never existed.

   The following are a few of the more popular business ethics texts which illustrate this view of ethical theory. Norman Bowie [*Business Ethics* (New Jersey, Prentice-Hall, 1982)], in discussing ethical theory, considers what he calls "both of the great traditions in ethical theory—the deontological and the utilitarian" (p. 10). Richard T. DeGeorge [*Business Ethics* (New York: Macmillan, 1982)] maintains that the two systems that have dominated ethical theory are teleological and deontological ethics (p. 37). Manuel G. Velasquez [*Business Ethics: Concepts and Cases* (New Jersey, Prentice-Hall, 1982)], in discussing ethical principles in business, emphasizes utilitarian standards, considerations of rights and duties, and standards of justice. That is, deontological as well as utilitarian theory should be used in business ethics.

3. Contemporary ethicists who discuss business ethics have also appealed to natural rights principles, e.g., Thomas Hobbes's principle of self-preservation or John Locke's principle of property (which includes self-preservation), or Rawlsian contract theory. Criteria for distinguishing moral and nonmoral situations are also thought to be required.

4. The virtue ethics movement is often traced back to works of Elizabeth Anscombe and Philippa Foot. Alasdair MacIntyre, however, appears to be the most influential virtue ethics theorist. MacIntyre, Anscombe, and Foot take a neo-Aristotelian approach to virtue ethics.

In the 1990s, there were a number of attempts to apply virtue ethics to business. The following are some examples. (Also see note 1.) Richard C. Bartlett ["Take the High Ground," *Executive Excellence*, II (July 1994): 18–19] maintains that leaders should be concerned with virtue ethics in molding an ethical corporate culture. In "Are Deontology and Teleology Mutually Exclusive?" [*Journal of Business Ethics* 13 (August 1994): 615–623], James E. Macdonald and Caryn L. Beck-Dudley argue, as I do, that there is too much emphasis in discussions of business ethics on the use of deontological and utilitarian theories and not enough stress on the usefulness of virtue ethics. Richard T. Green ["Character Ethics and Public Administration," *International Journal of Public Administration* 17 (November 1994): 2137–2164] presents an argument for the relevance of virtue (character) ethics to the responsibilities of public administrators and to "organizational economic arrangements." In "Virtue Ethics and Contractarianism: Towards a Reconciliation" [*Business Ethics Quarterly* 5 (April 1995): 297–312], Janet McCracken and Bill Shaw argue that any adequate model for business decision-making should be built upon an Aristotelian notion of virtue. They maintain that businesspeople should reflect upon the nature of the good and upon their own character. A contractarian-utilitarian model of (rational) moral decision-making in business is said to be inadequate because it neglects these Aristotelian consider-ations. This model should be combined with an ethics of virtue. Janet McCracken, William Martin and Bill Shaw ["Virtue Ethics and the Parable of the Sadhu," *Journal of Business Ethics* 17 (January 1998): 25–38] are critical, as I have been, of what has been called the "quandary ethics" approach to business ethics problems—the application of ethical rules to the ethical dilemmas or problems of business. The authors believe that an Aristotelian virtue ethic, which is character-based, should be emphasized in business ethics. Daryl Koehn ["A Role for Virtue Ethics in the Analysis of Business Practice," *Business Ethics Quarterly* 5 (July 1995): 533–539] argues that Aristotelian virtue ethics provides important insights into business practices, insights neglected by utilitarian and deontological ethics. John Dobson believes that virtue ethics provides the best ethical theory for professional ethics ["Ethics in Finance II," *Financial Analysts Journal* 53 (Jan/Feb 1997): 15–25]. He suggests that "A true professional is one who pursues the excel-lences, or internal goods, specific to his profession or practice." The reader may also be interested in my article, "Platonic Virtue Theory and Business Ethics," *Business and Professional Ethics Journal* 8, #4 (1990): 59–82.

5. William C. Frederick, *Values, Nature and Culture in the American Corporation* (New York: Oxford University Press, 1995), p. 219.

6. Frederick, p. 230. Similarly, Robert C. Solomon (in *Ethics and Excellence: Cooperation and Integrity in Business*), who argues for an Aristotelian approach to business ethics, says, "The two traditional ethical approaches [deontological ethics

and utilitarianism] have been criticized as clumsily irrelevant, or overly abstract for the particular situations faced by business managers, and for good reason" (p. 113).

7. However, I am not denying that virtue ethics theorists can be overly rigid, impractical, and unfair.

8. A corporate culture is defined in terms of the values that guide the conduct of the firm's members, and the culture is strong if these values are clearly visible and emphasized so that, as Terrence E. Deal and Allan A. Kennedy maintain, they give meaning and purpose to corporate activity [*Corporate Cultures: The Rites and Rituals of Corporate Life* (Reading, Mass.: Addison-Wesley Pub. Co., 1982), p. 5]. The basic values of a strong corporate culture guide its strategy and organization—they permeate the layers of the firm; generally, these shared values lead to shared beliefs. The basic values of a strong corporate culture are reinforced by stories about heroes and legends, corporate rites, rituals and symbols.

9. Solomon, *Ethics and Excellence: Cooperation and Integrity in Business*, see chapter 14.

10. I think that Solomon is right when he says that An Aristotelian view of business would insist that success and happiness in business should be commensurate with excellence. "To reward only results, to ignore the virtues that go into every effort," he says, "is to further the game and gambling aspect of business and discourage the pride and prosperity that in fact constitute its justification" (Solomon, *Ethics and Excellence: Cooperation and Integrity in Business*, p. 158).

11. Frederick, p. 232.

12. Frederick says, "Caring for one's fellow employees or for a firm's customers may count for much in one firm, while in another business more attention might be paid to simple instrumental ways of promoting the company's economizing goals without regard for the needs of others. As these signals are sent through perceptual pathways, they simultaneously help establish and reinforce ethically acceptable ways of behaving and making workplace decisions" (Frederick, p. 233).

13. "From Sicily to the Euxine, from Cyrene to Thrace, he [Aristotle] knows and can cite the constitutional development and the political vicissitudes of each state. Diogenes Laertius assigns to Aristotle 158 *Polities of States*" [Ernest Barker, *The Political Thought of Plato and Aristotle* (New York: Dover Publications, 1959), p. 210]. Ross says, "We feel in *Politics* IV.–VI. even more than elsewhere how completely he is master of the whole lore of the city-state, and how firmly his feet are planted on history" [W. D. Ross, *Aristotle* (London: Methuen and Co., 1923), p. 236].

14. Barker suggests that Aristotle should be called "physician in general to the States of Greece"; he is concerned with applying "the proper medicines for the diseases of actual states" (Barker, pp. 210, 212).

15. We may note in passing that some modern organizational theorists have recognized that there may not be one best model for all organizations. Frank Fischer and Carmen Sirianni [*Critical Studies in Organization and Bureaucracy* (Philadelphia: Temple University Press, 1984)] say, "Much [organizational] theory in recent years has tried to explain internal organizational change as a response or adjustment to environmental changes. The product of these efforts has been the development of 'contingency theory,' designed to show how different types of environments—open and closed, turbulent or placid—require different types of internal managerial structures. Therefore, some organizational environments dictate the introduction of hierarchical structures (of, say, scientific management), while others might require participatory models (of, say, human relations theory or organizational humanism)" (p. 9).

16. Thus Solomon, in *Ethics and Excellence: Cooperation and Integrity in Business*, is being Aristotelian, as he professes, by trying to improve business ethically from the inside. He says, "What a business ethicist can do is to enter into the business world and improve its perspectives and conceptions of its own activities" (p. 7).

17. In the *Politics*, Aristotle's notion of moral virtue—his doctrine of the mean—guides his discussion of political regimes from the most ideal to what he calls perverse forms of government. In an ideal society, the citizens are virtuous, and the more a political regime inclines citizens to be virtuous, the closer the regime is to an ideal form of government. Aristotle shows how applying the doctrine of the mean to the dominant political regimes—oligarchy (stressing wealth) and democracy (emphasizing freedom)—moderates their extreme tendencies and, therefore, inclines them more to virtue.

18. See Milton Friedman, "The Social Responsibility of Business is to Increase Profits," *New York Times Magazine*, Sept. 13, 1970. (This article has been reproduced in a number of business ethics anthologies.)

19. Points relating to Peters and Waterman can be found in their book, *In Search of Excellence: Lessons from America's Best-Run Companies* (New York: Harper and Row, 1982).

20. The organization man dominated American business in the 1950s and 1960s.

21. For Maccoby's views on the gamesman, as well as on the jungle fighter and the company man, see Michael Maccoby, *The Gamesman: The New Corporate Leaders* (New York: Simon and Schuster, 1976).

22. James D. Wallace, "Ethics and the Craft Analogy," in *Midwest Studies in Philosophy, Volume XIII, Ethical Theory: Character and Virtue*, eds. Peter A. French, Theodore E. Uehling, Jr., Howard K. Wettstein (Notre Dame, IN: University of Notre Dame Press, 1988), p. 224.

23. *Technē* requires a knowledge of the (end) product—its nature or form—so that the technician can work out the means to this end.

24. However, some *technai* require more of what *phronēsis* can provide than others. We might imagine a graded scale with *technai* such as grammar at one end—where knowledge of general rules is sufficient to apply to examples—and such *technai* as medicine, gymnastics, and navigation on the other—where the *technai* are not adequate to deal with the complexity of all individual cases; at this end, *phronēsis* is essential.

25. Aristotle says that temperance (*sōphrosynē*) is the preserver of *phronēsis* (NE 1140-b14–15).

26. The process by which a *phronimos* induces generalizations from the habitual experience of particular excellent acts may be analogous to the process of inducing general rules from experienced particulars. But the *phronimos* also develops a sensitivity, a perceptiveness, for ethically relevant particulars from the experience of such particulars (NE 1143b9–15, NE 1143a35–1143b5).

27. If our feelings or passions, like our appetites, are extreme, to use Aristotle's image, our aim is going to be off. Our feelings or passions cause us to interpret situations in a certain way. Thus, for example, a person who is cowardly will interpret certain situations as threatening when they are not, and an angry person will see insults where none were intended. *Phronēsis* depends upon virtue and virtue relates to feelings. The *phronimos* will have feelings—feelings aimed at a mean—which correctly interpret a situation, and he or she will appropriately respond to it. From the standpoint of moral education, the process of perceiving correctly depends upon moderating our passions so that our feelings are not extreme—excessive or deficient.

28. Edwin M. Hartman [*Organizational Ethics and the Good Life* (New York: Oxford University Press, 1996)] underscores the power of corporate influence on members of a firm. He says, "To the extent that the workplace has replaced other community institutions, organizations accumulate greater power to socialize. We think of religion as teaching people to strive to be a certain sort of person, to try to have the right dispositions. Now corporate culture performs that function" (p. 152).

29. A *technē*, for Plato and Aristotle, is a skill qua craft; thus, Wallace talks about a craft analogy. A technician uses, according to these philosophers, a system or method based upon rules of art. To make something in a workmanlike way (*technik-os*) is to work by the rules of the specific art. Gilbert Ryle appeals to this notion of

technē in his famous distinction between knowing that and knowing how. Although skillful performances are conducted without overtly referring to relevant rules or principles, skills are taught by providing pupils with what Ryle calls "the maxims and prescriptions of their arts" [Gilbert Ryle, The *Concept of Mind* (Harmondsworth, Penguin Books, 1949), p. 31]. Skills (know how) are often complex dispositions which involve observance "of rules or canons or application of criteria" (Ryle, p. 46). As Ryle maintains, this knowledge is clearly insufficient to master a skill—knowing how is not reducible to knowing that. Beginners at some skill, e.g., chess, consciously apply rules (which pertain to the movement of pieces), but as he suggests, once we become more proficient, we no longer think about the rules, and, indeed, we may not remember them. Since, as Ryle correctly suggests, the intelligence involved in intellectually grasping "prescriptions" is different from the intelligence and aptitude involved in putting prescriptions into practice, we may develop, with enough application, competence in the application of the requisite rules and principles, but without sufficient aptitude for the relevant know how, it is difficult to become very proficient or expert. Indeed, at these highest levels of skill, one may question whether or not rules and principles are even relevant. Herbert L. and Stuart Dreyfus [*Mind over Machine: The Power of Human Intuition and Expertise in the Era of the Computer* (New York: The Free Press, 1986)] argue that at the highest levels of skill, salient features related to a problem or situation are grasped intuitively by experience, not by applying rules or principles. No one would sensibly argue that a person who is proficient or expert at a skill applies rules consciously. But even the Dreyfuses maintain that the proficient performer looks at tasks from a specific perspective (point of view) and sometimes a specific goal (Dreyfuses, p. 32). How, then, is the skilled person not guided by principles, at least unconsciously? Indeed, they suggest that these "perspectives" may have to be evaluated when events or situations demand a change of perspective. While criticizing what they call the Platonic position—experts appeal implicitly (unconsciously) to rules or principles they use (Dreyfuses, p. 105)—they deny, in another breath, that their position can be proven because proficient and expert performers' judgments defy explanation (Dreyfuses, p. 36). They are correct, however, in suggesting that increased expertise involves greater ability or proficiency in dealing with particular cases, and this is what Aristotle argues. But even with the requisite experience one may, at least at times, fall short of expert performance. The (baseball) pitcher or batter and the golfer, for example, to be expert must exhibit touch or feel. The term "perception" must not be equated here with "seeing" alone. Sometimes touch or feel may escape the best pitcher, batter or golfer; but even if touch, feel, and perception in general cannot be reduced to applying rules or principles, and a batter, pitcher or golfer will not automatically regain proper feel or touch by a coach changing his or her mechanics, the principles of the mechanics and the knowledge involved are indispensable for "homing in" on the problem and making the necessary adjustments. Proficient and expert performers will exhibit greater precision and regularity than will persons whose mechanics are not as good or who lack requisite knowledge.

30. Joel Kupperman, "Character and Ethical Theory," in *Midwest Studies in Philosophy, Volume XIII, Ethical Theory: Character and Virtue*, eds. Peter A. French, Theodore E. Uehling, Jr., Howard K. Wettstein (Notre Dame, IN: University of Notre Dame Press, 1988), p. 116.

31. Kupperman, p. 120.

32. In his book, *Character* (New York: Oxford University Press, 1991), Joel Kupperman raises a similar issue about consequentialism. The difficulty of determining future consequences leads to a reliance on moral rules that generally have good consequences. Like Kant's ethics, he suggests, classical utilitarianism is "parasitic on a classification scheme drawn from traditional morality" and "on commonsense claims about the usual consequences of actions within these classifications" (Kupperman, pp. 83, 84).

33. Modern moral theory and classical moral theory are not mutually exclusive. The former, which emphasizes rules and principles, does pay some, but not overly much, attention to character development. The latter, does not totally neglect rules, but gives them a much reduced, subordinate role with respect to character development.

CHAPTER IV

An Aristotelian View of Ethically Responsible Management

Introduction

It is often argued that a view of managerial responsibility which is concerned with the impact of management decisions on stakeholders is more ethically viable than one which considers the impact of such decisions on shareholders alone. I agree with this position, but it is unclear how corporate managers should function as moral agents and determine what is good for the corporation as a whole. More specifically, it is unclear how managers can create a fair balance among the legitimate claims of the various constituencies which are impacted upon by management's decisions. In this chapter, I show how some of Aristotle's analysis in the *Nicomachean Ethics* and the *Politics* is helpful in both clarifying the central difficulty in determining a just distribution of corporate goods and in providing a plausible solution to this problem.

This chapter will illustrate themes for which I have argued. We shall see that an Aristotelian solution to determining a just distribution of corporate goods by corporate leaders depends upon dialectical skill. The reader may recall that the Socratic dialectician has knowledge of what is good for a whole as well as skill at implementing justice. In this chapter, I use Aristotle as a model of the practically wise person (*phronimos*) who, in tackling the problem of a just balance of legitimate claims to goods, balances idealism and realism as well as theory and practice. Thus, he illustrates points which were emphasized in the preceding chapters.

The Managerial Creed

If one takes either an Aristotelian or a Platonic approach to ethical corporate leadership, such leadership, like political statesmanship, would require a knowledge of the value principles that determine an organized whole to be good.[1] The view of ethical corporate leadership that I hold, then, requires a philosophical perspective, for the above perspective is essentially philosophical. Knowledge of what makes a whole good is derived from what the ancients call practical wisdom or *phronēsis*, and they consider this wisdom to be essential to ethics and politics.

Alfred N. Whitehead thinks that business leaders should understand the importance of a philosophical perspective. He maintains that managers require a quality he calls foresight.[2] Foresight as to the necessary changes that may have to be made in a corporation is based upon the habit of understanding basic principles—those which pertain to the outside environment and its values as well as those which apply to the internal workings of the corporation.[3]

Over forty years ago, a theory of corporate ethical responsibility called the managerial creed[4] was proposed as a position that is replacing the older and strictly economics oriented classical view (business has no ethical responsibilities other than to produce goods and services efficiently, make money for shareholders, and conduct business in a lawful manner).[5] The managerial creed states that managers are not merely responsible to shareholders. They should justly or fairly balance the legitimate, though often competing, claims of customers, employees, suppliers, and the general public, as well as shareholders; that is, managers should be concerned with stakeholders and not merely stockholders. The emphasis is both on a grasp of what is good for the whole and on managerial ethics. Such managers must appeal to some criterion of justice or fairness when balancing or mediating among the interests of those segments of the population that are seen to be affected substantially by the activities of the firm. Ethically, as applied to modern corporate business, this position is sounder than the classical view. The classical view is based upon *laissez-faire* theory, but this theory never was designed to apply to a world of large corporations. Oligopoly, and not a pluralistic system of small businesses, is more the order of the day. Yet, according to Leonard Silk and David Vogel (in their executive conferences), "the classical strain seemed dominant."[6] Therefore, it is not at all clear that the managerial creed is replacing the classical view.

In Chapter 2, we saw that Silk, Vogel and others have argued that the more myopic business leaders still refuse to see corporate business as something more than an economic institution, but, as Irving Kristol argues, this view, although traditional, is unacceptable given the power and impact of corporations on society. Because of this impact, they are expected to attend to the public interest. In this sense, corporate leaders must learn to think politically; they "have to learn to govern, not simply execute or administer."[7]

It is clear, therefore, that one major obstacle to corporate business's acceptance of this need to understand what is good for the whole is their overemphasis on economic concerns. However, corporate leaders' ignorance of what is good for the whole is, in part, a product of a preferred type of corporate leader—the financier. If this leader's basic concerns and expertise are confined to economics, then, as we noted in Chapter 2, noneconomic values will be transformed, by the method of cost/benefit analysis, into economic values.[8] This will not be done out of a "bad heart"; it will be a product of an ignorance of what is good for the whole and a consequence of putting a specialist, rather than a qualified generalist, in the position of running a firm. E. F. Schumacher puts the problem well when he suggests that with such a leader, "the higher is reduced to the level of the lower and the priceless is given a price."[9] Business is enormously simplified by reducing qualitative concerns to quantitative concerns, but only at the price of relieving oneself of basic responsibilities.[10]

It is no wonder, then, that talk about a managerial creed is often seen as a manipulative device of management.[11] The corporation often is perceived as having little time or inclination to dwell on the needs of the consumer or, in certain respects, on those of the employee when not viewed from the standpoint of increased productivity. In this context the managerial creed tends to sound like lip service, and corporate business's attempts to reduce doubts about its sense of ethical responsibility by creating images that counter these doubts do not seem to be doing it much good.[12]

Aside from the question of corporate acceptance of the managerial creed, there is still a question concerning how a manager, in this context, should function as an ethical agent, even if the managerial creed is considered morally preferable to the classical position. Peter F. Drucker agrees with the notion of balancing the interests of legitimate constituencies (the managerial creed), but he says that "no one tried to define what those best balanced interests were or should be, let alone how performance of this 'trustee' [management] could be defined or managed."[13]

Optimizing Political Justice: The Aristotelian *Phronimos* in Action

Let us assume the type of managerial leadership implied by the managerial creed. As suggested, this leader has a grasp of what is good for the whole and functions as a moral agent ought to function. What is necessary in order to know what is good for the corporation and to function as a moral leader?

We have seen that both Plato and Aristotle equate the capacity to determine what is good for a whole with practical wisdom. Plato, however, grounds the principle of practical wisdom in an idea (form) of the good itself. He believes that a partial human good can only be known to be good by knowing the human good as a whole, and this can only be known to be good by first knowing the good itself, which, in some way, is the ground of all Platonic forms (all Platonic knowledge). Aristotle criticizes this view. His important criticism, for our purposes, is that such an idea cannot serve as a guide for action. The good-in-itself, for example, will not serve the meteorologist or the doctor, for it will not help the former to predict good or bad weather; neither will it help the latter to discover what good health is. A theoretical investigation into the good itself seems far removed from determining the right thing to do in a concrete situation. Aristotle argues that actions refer to particulars. A doctor does not treat people in general; he treats *this* person and he does this given his knowledge of a healthy body, not some putative knowledge of an abstract good-in-itself. He would argue that the idea of a good-in-itself can no more guide the corporate statesman or the legislator than it can help the meteorologist or the doctor.[14]

It may be maintained, then, that a morally responsible corporate leader requires a set of rules or formulae that can be applied directly to specific cases to determine what is the right thing to do. In the preceding chapter, we have seen that Aristotle would argue that this opinion is mistaken, and it suggests an inadequate view of both moral agents and the practically wise persons.

We recall that, according to Aristotle, moral virtue is developed through habituation; we become virtuous by doing virtuous acts. Knowledge of the human good is essential for "like archers who have a mark to aim at," this knowledge provides a goal for guiding conduct (NE 1094a24–25). Therefore, legislators who "miss their mark"—by not forming morally virtuous habits in citizens—miss the opportunity of producing a good city (NE 1103b3–6). Although there is a right principle of conduct, ethics, by its nature, is imprecise. Therefore, there is no way of specifying a set of rules that can determine adequately right actions.

Assuming that an Aristotelian approach to ethical corporate leadership, which emphasizes moral virtue and practical wisdom rather than a rule-governed approach, is defensible—so that such a leader governs with knowledge of what is good for the whole and functions properly as a moral agent—it would seem that the Aristotelian position still leaves the corporate leader in the dark as to how to balance justly the competing claims of legitimate stakeholders. How much guidance are we given when we are told that the *phronimos* ascertains the mean by determining the right times, occasions, objects, people, motive, and manner for actions and that his or her determination rests upon perception?[15] A virtue approach to ethics, as Aristotle suggests, requires that one learns by positive experiences, and these experiences should be based upon an imitation of persons who are virtuous and practically wise. Assuming that Aristotle is a *phronimos*, how can he help us with the problem of justly balancing the competing claims of legitimate stakeholders?

It is first necessary to localize the central problem with respect to balancing justly legitimate, but competing, claims to goods. In considering this problem, it is helpful to return to Aristotle's criticism of Plato's idea of the good. If, according to Plato, there is an idea (form) of the good which is the cause of what is good in every good thing, then it would seem that the intrinsic goodness in all good things is the same. If every good is then commensurable with every other good, it should not be inordinately difficult to measure the degree of goodness (more or less goodness) in any putative good thing by comparing it with the ideal standard. If this is the case, it is no wonder that Plato emphasizes the theoretical problem of determining the good itself.

In Book III, Chapter 12 of the *Politics*, Aristotle argues against Plato's idea of the good by considering the good to which political science is directed—justice. He maintains that all people think that justice is a type of equality. The just distribution of political goods is relative to the just claims that can be made for them, and these claims depend upon the connection between the goods and the values on the basis of which the claims are made. Let us assume that superiority in birth and beauty are positive values just as excellence in flute-playing is; indeed, Aristotle believes that superiority in birth and beauty have greater intrinsic value than does excellence in flute-playing. Yet, the better flute should go to the better flute-player regardless of superior birth or beauty. With respect to a distribution of flutes, no superiority in birth or beauty can compensate for an inferiority in flute-playing. Similarly, one may argue that no amount of a nonpolitical good, e.g., musical ability, can equal a political good. Since it seems to be the case that different kinds of goods are incommensurable, Plato appears to be wrong.

Since the ethical problem of the corporate leader who manages in accordance with the managerial creed pertains to justice, let us elaborate upon the above position by considering Aristotle's theory of justice. Aristotle distinguishes between a broad and a narrow sense of "justice." In the broad sense, justice is equated with the goal of the laws—to produce actions conducive to the common welfare. Justice, in this sense, is identified with moral virtue in general insofar as morally virtuous conduct positively affects the welfare of others. Motives for different types of injustice can, thus, be quite various. There is also a sense of the term "justice," the one that most concerns us, which is identical to fairness. The ethical motive of an unjust as unfair act, according to Aristotle, is love of gain (*pleonexia*)—the desire to secure more than one's proper share of wealth, honor, office, or safety. Thus, the unjust person seeks an unfair share of goods that are sharable. Aristotle describes such goods as external goods; people compete for such goods and the more X gets, the less there is for Y. These goods should be distinguished from knowledge and moral virtue, for the more people there are who possess knowledge and moral virtue, the more they may be spread to others (NE 1169a6–11).

Since Aristotle believes that justice in the narrow sense is a virtue, for him, the fair is a mean; it is a mean between two unfair extremes.[16] What one can give may be of lesser, greater or equal value to what is received. Fairness is an equality between what is given and what is received. Just as the equal lies between the greater and the less, so the fair lies between what is unfair in excess and what is unfair in deficiency; that is, the fair lies between more than one merits and less than one merits. Aristotle analyzes fairness (with respect to the distribution of goods) as proportional equality—equality of ratios.[17] However, the goods to be rewarded are often different in kind, and we have seen that goods which are different in kind are incommensurable.

Aristotle illustrates this problem in the *Politics*. In political life, claims to offices or honors cannot be made on the basis of any value; they can only be made legitimately if the values are relevant to the offices and honors claimed. But even here there will be claims made on the basis of different values (what Aristotle calls "inequalities"). Therefore, we are faced with the problem of how comparatively to measure these values? Even if we agree that what is just (in distribution) should be according to merit, what is meritorious and to what degree may still be disputed. Aristotle suggests that oligarchs overemphasize wealth, aristocrats overemphasize virtue, while democrats assert that free people should share equally whatever the existing inequalities. Thus, each overemphasizes a specific value. How does one weigh (measure) the rival claims of wealth, virtue, and freedom?

Aristotle must face the problem of showing how justice in political matters is possible if justice is proportional equality, and such equality cannot be determined unless different values (different in kind) that contribute to the common good are somehow made commensurable. It is clear that there is no formula for solving this problem.[18] It is also clear that this problem is not only fundamental in politics, it is also central to managerial leadership which purports to be ethical.

Aristotle's solution to this problem, as one would suspect, involves his notion of the mean. After all, this is fundamental to the wisdom of the *phronimos*. And his solution is also practical, steeped in his reflections on politics. His solution is to give weight to the claims made by the various claimants (assuming that the values on the basis of which the claims are made are relevant to the claims on shares of the goods involved). Aristotle acknowledges that the principal values—wealth, virtue, and freedom—are all contributions to the common good, and, therefore, oligarchic, aristocratic, and democratic values make relevant claims on political goods such as offices or honors.[19] Justice, then, demands that different groups mutually recognize one another's claims (assuming they are legitimate claims) and, therefore, that each group would be willing to moderate its extreme claims and seek a balance among all the (legitimate) claims. Such a conciliatory and moderate attitude may be achieved by showing each of the claimants that on the basis of its own criterion or criteria, another faction(s) has a legitimate claim. Thus, the many, considered individually, can fail by the criteria of the oligarch and the aristocrat, but, Aristotle suggests, as a whole they can possess collective wealth and virtue that can be compared favorably with the wealth of the oligarch and the virtue of the aristocrat. Moreover, the virtuous may possess wealth and freedom while the wealthy may be both free and virtuous. In general, each class of claimant can be compared with others with respect to the criterion or criteria of the others. In this way, each claimant may admit that the others have legitimate claims. More specifically, since the claims of claimants may be turned against them, each class of claimant may be less inclined to push its own values exclusively and be more inclined to favor an attempt to balance the claims of the various claimants. In this way, the narrow self-interest of each claimant can be moderated and some notion of a common good, resulting from a balancing or harmonizing of claims (determining some sort of proportionality among the claims), may emerge. But, clearly, there is no formula, no mathematical procedure, for determining a fair balance among the claims, and it would also seem that abstract reasoning cannot yield a theoretical solution to the practical problem of determining just proportions. Specific examples of this problem should be considered case by case, and solutions should be determined by perceptions of the facts of the individual cases.

Aristotle might have drawn an analogy between a corporate statesman and a statesman as an arbiter among competing self-interested groups. According to Aristotle, a statesman would see the whole of which the partisans are parts.

Implementing the Managerial Creed

Having discussed Aristotle's analysis of the balancing of political stakeholder's claims to political offices and honors, we shall now turn to an application of his analysis to the problem of balancing corporate stakeholder's claims to the goods provided by corporations. Like oligarchs who overemphasize the value of wealth, businesspeople who support the classical position (which we have seen differs from the managerial creed) overemphasize the same value; that is, they consider the pursuit of profit for the benefit of shareholders as central to the function of the corporation and, thus, overemphasize the bottom line or so-called profit maximization. However, if one takes a just or fair position, clearly the value of the contributions of employees and consumers, as well as shareholders, to the corporation must be considered just as Aristotle acknowledges the values of wealth, virtue, and free-dom—i.e., the values of the oligarch, aristocrat, and democrat—to the city. We have seen that Aristotle argues that the extreme attitudes of claimants may be moderated by showing that, on the basis of their own criterion or criteria, another faction(s) has a legitimate claim to the goods that are sought. A particularly interesting point that is relevant to our concerns is his belief that although individually "the many" may be poorer and inferior in virtue to other constituents in the city, collectively their wealth and virtue can be compared favorably with the wealth of the oligarch and the virtue of the aristocrat. A similar situation obtains with regard to employees, especially in comparison with shareholders. Drucker says that in 1992, pension funds owned half of the share capital of the United States' large businesses and about the same amount of their fixed debts.[20] He maintains that the enormous pools of money in pension funds since the 1950s are greater than any capitalist of the past could command.[21] But the owners of pension funds are employees and future pensioners. Therefore, they are the owners of a great deal of "capital" without being capitalists. Ironically, argues Drucker, if socialism is defined as ownership of the means of production by employees, the United States is the most socialistic of all countries.[22] Thus, arguing as Aristotle would, by the very criterion of the classical position, a corporation should exist for the benefit of its employees every bit as much as for the benefit of its shareholders. Arguing in a manner analogous to the way Aristotle argues for the claims of "the many" vis-à-vis those of the wealthy, Drucker says, "collectively [through pension funds, mutual funds, retirement accounts, etc.] the employees own the means of production, [although] individually, few of them are wealthy."[23]

But the claims of employees, or at least many of them, can also be made on the basis of virtue—using the original meaning of virtue (*aretē*), human excellence. Drucker argues that not only do employees own a substantial part of the "means of production," they are also rapidly becoming the owners of the "tools of production" because knowledge has become the real capital of big business, and employees who are "knowledge workers," as he calls them, are thus the real "owners" of this capital.[24] We are told by Drucker, Thomas J. Peters, Robert H. Waterman, Jr. and many other contemporary management theorists that the self-development of workers and the consequent knowledge or skills attained are essential to the successful modern corporation. It would also seem that the satisfaction, pride in accomplishment, and sense of dignity derived from both the quality of their work and the possession of the "autonomy" with which to do their own work—which motivates them to pursue "excellence"—are basic to corporate productivity and therefore the bottom line. Thus, from the standpoint of both the classical position and the importance of "virtue," the claims of employees as stakeholders (on all corporate levels) cannot be minimized.

The consumer can claim the role of an important stakeholder on the basis of the corporate oligarch's position—a position which argues from the purpose of the corporation. It may be a fact that many businesspeople believe, as does the corporate oligarch, that the goal of business is to maximize profit (for the shareholders), but it is not clear that this should be the goal of business. Drucker believes that professionals must provide society with something considered valuable or good. Indeed, Drucker maintains that the purpose of business is to provide customers with goods and services they consider a "value." He says, "What the customer thinks he is buying, what he considers 'value,' is decisive—it determines what a business is, what it produces and whether it will prosper."[25] Of course, profit is essential to business, but Drucker maintains that this is because it is the basic test of the performance of a business, and it places a limit on what a business can do. What is called profit in the short run turns out to be something that pays for the cost of doing business in the longer run (it determines what a business can do). An emphasis on short term profit can create a conflict between ethical responsibility and business goals, but only profit can secure the future of business and allow it to make a social contribution as well as meet possible ethical obligations, e.g., supply more and better jobs, secure or increase the quality of a product, and pay for certain of society's services.

Although Drucker's position is controversial, some arguments can be used in its defense. Business, as the motto of the Harvard Business School tells us, wants to be considered a profession. Plato shows that moneymaking is not a defining characteristic of what we might call a profession.[26] Plato suggests that by analogy with standard professions, professional knowledge should be used to help persons for whom the professional provides a service (see *Republic* 341c–342e). Generally, every institutionalized profession exists for the sake of serving society. Thus, Drucker can dialectically refute the businessperson who wants to be considered a professional but also wants to define the goal of business as maximizing profit. Moreover, as Richard T. De George says, "Business is a social enterprise. Its mandate and limits are both set by society."[27] If a business is so concerned with maximizing profit that it acts in an ethically irresponsible way, society must deem such a purpose illegitimate, even if business management posits this goal. If business receives its mandate from society, it must be because society views it as an institution that provides people with desirable material goods and services and thus we are back to Drucker's position.

Madison and Aristotle on Maximizing Political Justice

It might be helpful to compare James Madison's famous attempt to maximize political justice with Aristotle's. Madison, in *Federalist #10*, mentions the common complaint "that the public good is disregarded in the conflicts of rival parties, and that measures are too often decided, not according to the rules of justice and the rights of the minor party, but by the superior force of an interested and overbearing majority."[28] Madison agrees with Aristotle that people are biased judges when their own interests are involved, and this produces a "factious spirit" in which self-interest is pitted against the rights of others and the common good. Madison argues that human beings have a factious nature which is fueled by unequal distribution of property. Thus, as Aristotle suggests, the few (wealthy) and the many (poor) are the basic contending factions, and Aristotle and Madison agree that justice demands that a balance be struck between contending parties,[29] but in reality the more powerful party pre-vails—might makes right.

Madison argues that if the causes of factions cannot be removed,[30] we should investigate how their effects can be controlled. He maintains that moral or religious persuasion is not sufficient to control factions when opportunities for injustice present themselves. Instead of appealing to rational persuasion, as Aristotle does, Madison emphasizes the splintering of power as much as possible so that it is not overly concentrated in one faction, even a majority faction. Thus, Madison argues that the greater the number of citizens and extent of territory, the greater the variety of parties (and therefore interests) so that in a representative republic it will be less likely that some constant majority exists or even where it does, that it can be discovered easily. This solution is reflected at the level of government in the separation of powers (checks and balances), including legislative checks and balances between the Senate and the House. It may be noted that the diversity of interests among factions and the consequent advantages from the standpoint of justice also are implicit in Adam Smith's economic theory—in division of labor. Of course, Smith, like Madison, also emphasizes, as central to *laissez-faire* theory, the splintering of power—in this case, economic power.

Aristotle's method of maximizing political justice differs from Madison's in that it is based upon rational persuasion and bears some similarity to Socratic method. We saw that fundamental to Aristotle's method of creating balance (or justice) among contending factions is the ability of the *phronimos* to persuade each of the rival factions that on the basis of its own criterion or criteria, another faction(s) has a legitimate claim to the desired goods. Thus, like Socrates, Aristotle appeals to the premises that people are willing to admit and he shows that the premises they hold may not be as favorable to them as they think. In this way, the unjust effects of narrow self-interest can be moderated and a fairer distribution of goods among contending factions is made possible.

Notes

1. Unlike Plato, however, Aristotle does not think that the statesman's knowledge of the good city or the good person requires metaphysical knowledge, that is, knowledge of the total scheme of things and people's places in that scheme.

2. Aristotle maintains that we apply the term "practical wisdom" to one who has foresight with respect to his or her own life [*Nicomachean Ethics* (NE) 1141-a29–31].

3. Alfred N. Whitehead, *Adventures in Ideas* (New York: Mentor Book, 1955), Chapter 6. This point of view is also emphasized in business theory, for example, by George C. Lodge. As I mentioned in Chapter 1, he maintains that in order to deal adequately with the realities of corporate business, a manager must be willing "to confront manifold change openly and with a breadth of vision.... He must see his task as a general not a specific one.... He is an integrator, a synthesizer, responsible for the whole and capable of perceiving the whole within and without" [George C. Lodge, "Business and the Changing Society," in *Issues in Business and Society*, eds. George A. Steiner and John F. Steiner, 2nd ed. (New York: Random House, 1977), p. 144].

4. Francis X. Sutton, Seymour E. Harris, Carl Haysen, and James Toben, *The American Business Creed* (Cambridge: Harvard University Press, 1956). The term often used is corporate social responsibility.

5. See note 40, p. 48 or note 18, p. 80.

6. Leonard Silk and David Vogel, *Ethics and Profits: The Crisis of Confidence in American Business* (New York: Simon and Schuster, 1976), p. 137.

7. Irving Kristol, *Two Cheers for Capitalism* (New York: Mentor Book, 1978), p. 71. Donaldson says the following about the corporation. "It is a state within a state, and it competes on some levels even with the government in the management of social and economic events. The corporation, like the government, has a citizenry from which it commands loyalty, and this citizenry includes shareholders, suppliers, and employees." Thomas Donaldson, *Corporations and Morality* (Englewood Cliffs, New Jersey: Prentice-Hall, 1982), pp. 8–9.

8. E. F. Schumacher, *Small is Beautiful: Economics as if People Mattered* (New York: Perennial Library, 1973), p. 45.

9. Schumacher, p. 46.

10. Schumacher, p. 44.

11. While presenting the image of a well-intentioned manager, one could justify, for example, not giving employees a raise by maintaining that the increase would have to be passed on to consumers or would be contrary to the interests of the shareholders who would not accept it. Generally, each group could be manipulated with arguments of this sort, one group being played off against another.

12. The following is possibly a more realistic, and certainly a more pessimistic, picture of how a managerial creed would work. Different groups affected by corporate decisions will exert different, and often incompatible, pressures on management. Unions want higher wages, etc., shareholders want higher dividends, consumers want lower prices. In practice, might makes right; that is, management will yield in proportion to the greater force.

13. Peter F. Drucker, *Post-Capitalist Society* (New York: Harper Collins, 1993), p. 79.

14. In the *Nicomachean Ethics*, Aristotle uses the criteria of that which is perfect or complete (*to haplōs teleion*), self-sufficiency (*to autarkes*), and that which is desired as a final end (*to teleion*) as ideas which regulate inquiry into the nature of happiness—*eudaimonia*—(NE 1097a3–1097b22). The above criteria for the human good, as R. Hackforth suggests, are based upon what Plato says about the human good in the *Philebus* (20d–22b). [*Plato's Philebus*, trans. with intro. and commentary by R. Hackforth (Cambridge: Cambridge University Press, 1945), p. 32.] At *Philebus* 20d, Socrates considers criteria for determining the human good. It must be perfect or complete (*to teleion*)—and therefore a final end—adequate or sufficient (*ti hikanōn*), and it is pursued (desired) by all who recognize it (*to*

hairetos). The first two criteria are connected in that the perfect is self-sufficient; it has "no need of anything else to be added to it" (*Philebus* 20e).

Since Aristotle criticizes the Platonic idea of the good, why should he think that his own practical philosophy, which investigates the human good by using Plato's criteria in the *Philebus* for determining the human good, is practical? Plato, here, is considering criteria for the human good and not the idea of the good-in-itself. Secondly, Insofar as Plato's investigation aims at theoretical knowledge and Aristotle's at action, Aristotle does have a point. It should be emphasized, however, that as abstract as Plato's investigation in the *Philebus* is, Aristotle, himself, shows (in the *Nicomachean Ethics*) how Plato's criteria for the human good determine morally virtuous conduct and contemplation as the human good (*eudaimonia*), and knowledge of the human good, Aristotle thinks, is indispensable for practical wisdom.

15. Aristotle says, "With a view to action experience seems in no respect inferior to art, and men of experience succeed even better than those who have theory without experience.... The reason is that experience is knowledge of individuals, art of universals, and actions and productions are all concerned with the individual" (*Metaphysics* 981a12ff).

16. Aristotle says that justice is not a mean in the way in which the other virtues are. The other virtues lie between two vices, but there is only one vice corresponding to justice—injustice, which is an excess. The deficiency would involve an agent giving more of a good to another and taking less for himself, but generosity is not a vice.

17. See *Nicomachean Ethics*, Book V for Aristotle's discussion of justice.

18. Solomon agrees that the use of *phronēsis*—which he translates as good judgment—to solve problems of justice does not involve a mechanical procedure. He says, "There is *no* (non-arbitrary) mechanical decision procedure for resolving most disputes about justice, and what is required, in each and every particular case, is the ability to balance and weigh competing concerns and come to a 'fair' conclusion" [Robert C. Solomon, "Corporate Roles, Personal Virtues, Moral Mazes: An Aristotelian Approach to Business Ethics," in *Business Ethics and the Law*, eds. C. A. J. Coady and C. J. G. Sampford (Sidney: The Federal Press, 1993), p. 40].

19. Books VII and VIII of the *Politics* consider the construction of an ideal state. The goal of the state, for Aristotle, is the same as that of the individual—*eudaimonia* or happiness (the human good). *Eudaimonia*, as the *Nicomachean Ethics* tells us, is based on virtuous activities. Virtue, then, is the qualification for ruling in Aristotle's ideal state. Since the citizens of this ideal state are virtuous, and Aristotle thinks that it is unlikely that some one of the citizens is so superior to the others that he should be the permanent ruler, each citizen may rule when he reaches the appropriate age. It might seem, then, that Aristotle is denying that freedom and wealth are bases for political participation, for virtue alone appears to be the qualification for such

participation. To deal with this issue properly, one should distinguish between Aristotle's ideal state—which, as he says, "is an aspiration only" (*Politics* 1295-a29)—and his version of the best practicable state (*Politics* 1295a25–31), for it is this latter conception that should concern us most if we are to apply Aristotelian political ideas to a study of business ethics. Aristotle calls the best practicable state, polity, and, as W. D. Ross says, "the characteristic of polity is that it takes account both of wealth and of free status in its distribution of office" [*Aristotle* (London: Methuen and Co., 1949), p. 259]. Polity is a mean between the extreme claims of oligarchy and democracy; in this state, the middle class has the political power. Middle class rule, which embodies a moderation of the extreme claims of oligarchy and democracy, is inherently temperate rule and thus disposes citizens toward virtue (see *Politics* 1295b4–9). Indeed, in helping to dispose citizens toward virtue, polity aims at the good of the state, *eudaimonia*, for, as we have said, Aristotle believes that happiness is constituted essentially of virtuous activities. Therefore, according to Aristotle, the claims of oligarchy (wealth), democracy (freedom), and aristocracy (virtue) can be given appropriate weight within the context of his best practicable state.

Given the nature of Aristotle's ideal state, it is possible that a reader familiar with Aristotle may raise the following objection to the applicability of Aristotle's political theory to business ethics. The legislators of Aristotle's ideal state will mold the citizens of this state so that the human good, the practice of virtue, is desired (*Politics* 1337a19–23). Such a political system is much more intrusive, more concerned with molding opinions, than are democratic systems. Therefore, it might be argued that given the fact that our political system is democratic, his antidemocratic position makes the application of his political theory to the problems of business ethics, as business ethics is practiced in countries like our own, inappropriate. I think that an answer to this objection should be based on Aristotle's distinction between an ideal state, which "is an aspiration only," and a best practicable state—polity. Although we have seen that polity is a compromise between the claims of oligarchy and democracy—wealth and freedom—Aristotle suggests that it inclines more towards democracy (*Politics* 1293b33–36). Therefore, if we are to concern ourselves with the application of political theory to the problems of business ethics and such a theory should consider "the best constitution for most states, and the best life for most men, neither assuming a standard of virtue which is above ordinary persons, nor an education which is exceptionally favored by nature and circumstances, nor yet an ideal state which is an aspiration only, but having regard to the life in which the majority are able to share, and to the form of government which states in general can attain" (*Politics* 1295a25–31), polity may well fill the bill, and it should not rub against the grain, at least not inordinately, of our democratic sentiments.

20.   Drucker, p. 6.

21.   Drucker, p. 75.

22.   Drucker, p. 6.

23. Drucker, p. 67.

24. Drucker, p. 8.

25. Peter F. Drucker, *The Practice of Management* (New York: Harpers Row, 1954), p. 37.

26. Actually, the term Plato uses is *"technai."* As we have seen, this term is usually translated as skill or craft. However, the Liddell and Scott Greek dictionary suggests that, for Plato, to learn a *technē* is to learn to do something professionally.

27. Richard T. De George, *Business Ethics* (New York: Macmillan, 1982), p. 8.

28. Alexander Hamilton, John Jay, James Madison, *The Federalist,* intro. Edward Mead Earle (New York: The Modern Library, 1937), p. 54.

29. It should be noted that throughout *Federalist #10*, Madison is concerned with creating a proper balance or proportion among factions, and in one place he refers explicitly to the doctrine of the mean (Hamilton, Jay, Madison, p. 60).

30. He believes that as long as one values liberty and dislikes conformity, factions cannot be eliminated.

CHAPTER V

Emotions, Rationality, and Business Ethics

Introduction

As Robert C. Solomon suggests, the standard version of the philosopher's view of reason and the passions—with which he disagrees—is that reason rather than the passions differentiates human beings from the lesser creatures in creation. The passions must be controlled by reason, for they are dangerous and disruptive forces which can confuse reason and lead it astray. "The wisdom of reason against the treachery and temptations of the passions," he says, "has been the central theme of Western Philosophy."[1] Although the passions can be dangerous and disruptive forces, the above view underestimates the importance of the passions in life and fails to consider their relevance to the proper functioning of practical reason.[2] It is this latter point I wish to develop in the first section of this chapter.[3]

In Chapter 3, I attempted to show that Aristotelian ethics exhibits a greater balance between theory and practice than does modern ethical theory, which often relies on teleological and/or deontological principles and rules. I argued that although modern moral theory is useful in business ethics, the neglect of Aristotelian *phronēsis*—which includes moral virtue—prevents the moral agent from adequately mediating between the rules and/or principles suggested by modern ethicists and moral problems. In this chapter, I shall offer scientific evidence as well as philosophical reflections to support the position that Aristotelian virtue ethics provides a better account of ethical decision-making—and therefore ethical practice—than does modern ethical theory. The arguments are based upon showing that emotions and feelings are indispensable to the proper functioning of practical reason.

Ironically, teleological/deontological *action*-based theories, in themselves, do not provide adequate explanations for sound moral decisions. Antonio R. Damasio's examination of the emotional impairment of a person called Elliot—considered in Section 2 of this chapter—shows that he is capable of sophisticated abstract moral thinking, whether teleological or deontological, but because of his emotional impairment, his decision making is ineffective, poor, or nonexistent. Thus, the ability to think clearly in accordance with either or both of these theories is insufficient to determine sound moral decisions and to guide moral action.

Damasio shows that what is lacking in teleological and/or deontological moral theories is an understanding of the central role emotion—he uses the term "somatic markers"—plays in rational decision-making. Damasio's reflections and the similar thoughts of Ronald de Sousa, discussed in Section 2, are shown, in Section 3, to support a character- or virtue-based ethics; this type of ethical theory takes seriously the place of emotions in practical reasoning.[4] The implications for business ethics are clear. Some form of what is called virtue ethics must play an indispensable role in any discussion of theories of ethical decision-making in business or, more generally, in practical ethics. Thus, modern moral theorists who, in writing on ethical decision-making in business, rely exclusively on teleological and/or deontological theory or, negatively, neglect virtue ethics are providing the subject of business ethics with inadequate theory.

In Section 3 of this chapter, I follow the lead of Damasio and de Sousa; I argue that Aristotle's theory of ethical decision-making fits well with Damasio's inferences from his experimental findings and de Sousa's reflections on emotions and reasoning. Aristotle's theory of moral virtue offers a plausible account of the proper nurturing of emotions. It makes central Damasio's point that emotions or feelings should be properly developed so as to "point us in the proper direction" and "take us to the appropriate place in a decision-making space" (see note 10). Once an area of plausible alternatives has been properly delimited, practical wisdom can make a correct choice.

In the final section, I show that emotions are indispensable to the standard view of objective reasoning. I also show, using Robert H. Frank's examples, that emotions can help to resolve certain ethical dilemmas and therefore certain ethical business dilemmas.

Emotions and Practical Reasoning

In Chapter 1 of *Descartes' Error*, Antonio R. Damasio discusses the well-known case of Phineas P. Gage.[5] In 1848 Gage, a construction foreman, had the misfortune of having an iron rod propelled (by means of an explosion) through his left cheek, piercing the base of the skull, traversing the front of his brain, and exiting through the top of his head. Remarkably, although Gage lost his left eye, two months after the accident he was pronounced cured. He not only regained his physical strength, his sense perception was intact and his physical equilibrium and dexterity, facility with speech and language were fine. Even his abstract intellectual abilities were intact. What was impaired, however, was his capacity to make rational decisions.

Before the accident, Gage was admired for his "well-balanced mind," "temperate habits," and fine character; he was also considered the most efficient and capable employee in his company.[6] After the accident, however, the balance between his intellectual and emotional capacities was destroyed. Prior to his accident Gage knew

> all he needed to know about making choices conducive to his betterment. He had a sense of personal and social responsibility, ... cared for the quality of his work, and attracted the admiration of employers and colleagues. He was well adapted in terms of social convention and appears to have been ethical in his dealings. After the accident, he no longer showed respect for social convention; ethics were violated; the decisions he made did not take into account his best interest.... There was no evidence of concern about his future, no sign of forethought.[7]

Damasio believes that Gage's case shows that ethical activity, planning for the future, conventionally proper social behavior, and making decisions which are personally advantageous require both knowledge of rules and strategies and intact brain functions relating to emotion and feeling.[8] Although Damasio agrees with the common wisdom that emotions can bias reasoning, he also maintains, and this is a central contention, "that certain aspects of the process of emotion and feeling are indispensable for rationality.[9] At their best, feelings point us in the proper direction, take us to the appropriate place in a decision-making space, where we may put the instruments of logic to good use."[10]

In order to substantiate his opinions about Gage, Damasio considers "a modern Phineas Gage," a patient of Damasio's, whom he calls Elliot. Elliot had a tumor which was compressing his frontal lobes—considerable damage was done to the ventromedial sector of his frontal cortices. The removal of the tumor and the damaged frontal lobe tissue left him, as did the accident to Gage, with a marked change in personality. He remained coherent, smart, and knowledgeable; generally, his skills and memory were unchanged.[11] However, after the operation, the effects he felt as the tumor grew—inability to concentrate, loss of a sense of responsibility, and an inability to complete and correct his work—remained. Although he was able to perform very circumscribed tasks well, he lost all sense of priorities and was unable to direct his activities effectively (towards appropriate goals). Generally, this otherwise healthy and intelligent person could no longer function as an effective social being. Before he felt the effects of the tumor, however, he had been a good husband, father, and a role model for younger siblings and colleagues.

In order to understand Elliot's disease better, he was subjected to a battery of tests; they showed that his mental functions were all normal or above normal. At this point in his investigation, Damasio begins to sniff out the problem when he notices that he was more pained by Elliot's stories than Elliot was. Basically, Elliot lacked emotion. Elliot, himself, recognized that he was not emotionally affected by human tragedy in the way he was before his illness. "We might summarize Elliot's predica-ment," says Damasio, "as *to know but not to feel.*"[12]

Elliot was tested to determine whether or not his decision-making failures were due to lost knowledge of social rules or principles.[13] This question could not be answered in Gage's case. It was shown that his failure was not due to the loss of such knowledge. The tests that were given to Elliot—relating to ethical dilemmas and financial questions—showed that his capacity to bring to mind alternative options to "social situations" and to determine the consequences of these options was not impaired. He was also able to conceptualize means for achieving social goals as well as being able to predict the probable results of social situations. "The findings indicated clearly that damage to the ventromedial sector of the frontal lobe did not destroy the records of social knowledge as retrieved under the conditions of the experiment."[14] Damasio concludes that Elliot's appropriate responses to the test questions indicate that there was a dissociation between "real-life failure and laboratory normalcy."[15]

How can one explain the discrepancy between his normal and superior scores on the above tests and his real life ineptitude at decision-making? Damasio maintains that Elliot's demonstrated social knowledge and his ability to access it in test conditions did not translate into the ability to make reasonable real life choices. Elliot, himself, admitted that although he was able to conjure up options for action out of his "rich imagination," he did not know how to choose among the options; that is, he either was unable to choose effectively, or he chose badly, or not at all. Damasio attributes Elliot's failings to the "cold-bloodedness" of his reasoning, which prevented him from assigning different values to different options and, consequently, making it most difficult for him to decide among the options.[16]

The cases of Gage, Elliot, and others who have been similarly impaired show that deficiencies in personal decision-making are not necessarily accompanied by deficiencies in the nonpersonal domain. This is supported by observations of human behavior. For example, we know or have heard or read about creative scientists and artists who are inept in the personal and social realms. It is in these areas that the greatest uncertainty and complexity arise.[17]

With reference to practical reasoning about social and personal problems, Damasio distinguishes between two views—the "high reason view," which he criticizes, and his own position, the "somatic-marker hypothesis." The former, rationalist, position—which, according to Damasio, has been championed by Plato,[18] René Descartes, Immanuel Kant, and others—maintains that "formal logic will, by itself, get us to the best available solution for any problem."[19] This view includes the belief that the rational process which leads to the best results suppresses emotions. To use business parlance, one should consider the alternative possibilities and perform a cost/benefit analysis of each of them. For example, says Damasio, according to this view, one should "consider the consequences of each option at different points in the projected future and weigh the ensuing losses and gains."[20] Against this view of rationality, he raises the following objection—one familiar from critics of utilitarianism and, more generally, ethical consequentialism. At best, a decision will take an inordinately long time; at worst, you will not make a decision because you will get lost in the complexity of your calculations. He also notes that there will be an excessively large number of items to hold in memory for comparison. "In the end," says Damasio, "if purely rational calculation is how your mind normally operates, you might choose incorrectly and live to regret the error, or simply give up trying, in frustration."[21] Ironically, Damasio suggests that this "cool" strategy defended by rationalists relates more to the way the Gages and Elliots process decisions than to the way normal people usually operate.[22]

Damasio's position, the somatic-marker hypothesis,[23] includes emotional reactions in the rational process which controls the number of alternatives considered; these emotional reactions make the decision-making process more manageable. Damasio suggests that, on this view, before we apply any kind of cost/benefit analysis to the many alternative possibilities—he calls them scenarios—we should pay attention to the unpleasant gut feelings which are associated with options that fleetingly cross our mind, options which we sense lead to bad results. A somatic marker functions as "an automated alarm signal," which limits the alternatives among which we will make a choice. Somatic markers can also be positive, in which case they function as "beacons of incentive."[24] As secondary emotions,[25] they are learned responses to possible alternatives. Rational choice, e.g., by means of cost/benefit analysis, is made much more manageable after somatic markers drastically limit the choices.[26] "Somatic markers," he maintains, "probably increase the accuracy and efficiency of the decision process."[27]

The above theory is made more complicated by the fact that negative and positive somatic markers must be considered together. Thus, for example, taking a pay cut or having working hours increased will probably be associated with an unpleasant feeling, but if we believe that what we are doing will lead to a future advantage, the positive somatic marker will override the tendency to decide against the painful options.

About seven years before the publication of *Descartes' Error*, Ronald de Sousa, writing as a philosopher rather than a neurologist, developed a theory about the relation of emotions to reasoning, especially ethical reasoning, which has striking similarities to Damasio's position.[28] De Sousa raises the question, what is the role of emotions in relation to rational behavior and belief?[29] To answer this question, he considers what he calls "the philosopher's frame problem"—how to make use of the vast amount of knowledge we possess, and how to avoid what we don't need. To make effective use of this knowledge, we must determine what he calls salience—"what to notice, what to attend to, what to inquire about."[30] Logic alone cannot ascertain salience; emotions, however, do determine salience.[31]

In considering the issue of salience, de Sousa mentions an illustration given by Daniel C. Dennett,[32] which is reminiscent of the problem of inaction Damasio considers in his discussion of Elliot. Dennett imagines a robot which is informed of a bomb that will go off in a hangar in which the robot is housed. Even after the robot is instructed to draw inferences from its vast supply of information, it is lost in computation, considering every possible implication. As one might suspect, it is still computing long after an action should have been taken. The robot is then instructed to ignore irrelevant implications. De Sousa quotes Dennett:

> They were surprised to see it [the robot] sitting, Hamlet-like, outside the room containing the ticking bomb.... 'Do something!' they yelled at it. 'I am,' it retorted, 'I'm busily ignoring some thousands of implications I have determined to be irrelevant....' But the bomb went off.[33]

As de Sousa says,

> What gives rise to the philosopher's frame problem is that we need to know whether a consequence will turn out to be relevant *before drawing it*. If it is

relevant and we have not retrieved it, we may act irrationally. But if it is irrelevant and we have already drawn it, we have already wasted time.[34]

De Sousa gives emotion a role in practical reasoning that is strikingly similar to the role Damasio gives to it.

> When the calculi of reason have become sufficiently sophisticated, they would be powerless in their own terms, except for the contribution of emotion. For emotions are among the mechanisms that control the crucial factor of salience, among which would otherwise be an unmanageable plethora of objects of attention, interpretations, and strategies of inference and conduct.[35]

Damasio understands that not only, in the way described above, are emotions essential to the proper functioning of practical reason, the human passion for reason is itself an indispensable aid to reason; he maintains that both theoretical and practical reason require this passion for mastering reasoning skills.[36] Scheffler elaborates on the importance of emotions to the rational life. The rational life, he tells us, presupposes certain emotional dispositions,

> for example, a love of truth and a contempt for lying, a concern for accuracy in observation and inference, and a corresponding repugnance at error in logic or fact. It demands revulsion at distortion, disgust at evasion, admiration of theoretical achievement, respect for considered arguments of others. Failing such demands, we incur rational shame; fulfilling them makes for rational self-respect.[37]

Generally, he suggests that a rational life demands a rational character just as a moral life demands a moral character. The right emotions should be directed towards the right things in the right way. A rational character, says Scheffler, "monitors and curbs evasions and distortions, it combats inconsistency, unfairness to facts, and wishful thinking.... It works for a balance in thought, an epistemic justice...."[38]

If emotions guide processes of practical reasoning, de Sousa suggests correctly that they can guide these processes propitiously or they can distort them. It is clear, then, that for the purpose of ethical reasoning, emotions must be properly developed. Damasio agrees; he maintains that most somatic markers used in rational decision-making are developed by education and socialization.[39] Without discussing the issue of character development, Damasio nonetheless recognizes that emotional reactions (somatic signals) can bias reasoning. He gives examples of obedience, conformity, and self-esteem drives.[40] If moral character is an indispensable aid to moral reasoning, the negative and positive somatic markers that are developed by moral education should aid rather than bias moral reasoning.

From a moral standpoint, then, the issue concerns the development of moral character or moral virtue. As de Sousa suggests, emotions are central to what he calls "the ethical conduct of life."[41] "This," he says correctly, "was obvious to Aristotle, for whom moral education consisted essentially in the education of the emotions."[42]

Aristotelian Virtue Ethics and Ethical Decision-Making

My discussion in Section 2 of this chapter has an important implication for business ethics. If what Damasio and de Sousa maintain is correct, a character- or virtue-based ethics—one which takes seriously the proper habituation of the emotions or passions—is indispensable for practical (and therefore business) ethics, for it is indispensable for properly comprehending ethical decision-making. Damasio and de Sousa think that Aristotle's ethics is helpful in understanding the place of the emotions in ethical reasoning, and I agree. Moreover, as we have seen in Chapter 3, Aristotle offers a theory of ethical decision-making that can be most helpful to business ethics theorists.

Since, in Chapter 3, I presented an Aristotelian theory of ethical choice or decision-making—a theory which compensates for difficulties in modern moral theories—I shall not repeat my discussion here. I should show, however, that Aristotle's theory of choice or decision-making accords well with the positions of Damasio and de Sousa.

As de Sousa suggests, Aristotle believes that moral education is an education of the emotions. Aristotle maintains that we should be brought up to delight in and be pained by the things that we ought [*Nicomachean Ethics* (NE) 1104b12–13]. Generally, we believe that we experience pleasurable or painful sensations when we are stirred by related emotions. Aristotle uses the term "passions" to refer to emotions that are accompanied by pleasure and pain (NE 1105b22–23), and he believes that pleasures and pains are the essential concerns of moral upbringing.

Aristotle defines the moral virtues in terms of character states, and he says that character states pertain to "the things in virtue of which we stand well or badly with reference to the passions" (NE 1105b25–26). We saw that, according to Aristotle, our passions or emotions can be extreme; that is, they can be either deficient or excessive. Moral virtue involves an habituation to an intermediate or mean position with reference to our emotions. When a morally virtuous person acts, he or she makes choices which reflect emotions that are balanced or duly proportioned. The Aristotelian moral person, then, is armed with a knowledge of virtue—a knowledge of different means between extremes—which are indeterminate with reference to particulars; we have seen that the mean cannot be determined mathematically—it is imprecise—and it is relative to individuals. *Phronēsis*, we recall, determines how this indeterminate mean is to be applied to particulars by choosing the right times, occasions, objects, people, motive (choosing virtuous actions for their own sakes), and manner (NE 1106b20–23). The *phronimos's* judgments are based upon perceptions or insights and are not easy to make (NE 1109a24–29).

It is clear that Aristotle does take account of the importance of emotions in considering moral choice or decision. His view, then, accords in principle with Damasio's and de Sousa's conclusions.

In Chapter 3, we saw that Aristotle suggests that knowledge of human virtue (right principles of conduct) is essential for "like archers who have a mark to aim at," this knowledge provides a goal for guiding conduct (NE 1094a24–25). Thus, like an archer, a morally virtuous person will score a better hit by recognizing the direction in which he or she must look and the things to which she must pay attention. But we saw that the practically wise person (the *phronimos*) does not hit the ethical mark by some art (*technē*) or by following some rule. Moral virtue provides the *phronimos* with a disposition to aim at proper human goals and to consider the particularities of a given problem in the light of these goals.

Aristotle's position is very reminiscent of Damasio's view. You may recall that Damasio maintains that when feelings are properly nurtured they "point us in the proper direction, take us to the appropriate place in a decision-making space, where we may put the instruments of logic to good use" (see note 10). Thus, the moral virtues provide the essential somatic markers which effectively delimit the area of plausible alternatives in which, according to Aristotle, *phronēsis* can make a proper choice.

In Chapter 3, I argued that Aristotelian *phronēsis*—which we have seen is intimately related to good character—is necessary to perceive adequately morally salient factors that are involved in morally problematic situations; it was also seen to be necessary to perceive certain situations as morally problematic or even as involving something of moral significance. In connection with de Sousa's notion of salience—what to notice, attend to, and inquire about—one may note that he too believes that character is logically tied to moral perception and therefore to moral judgment. According to de Sousa, whether or not we notice or attend to some salient moral feature of a situation depends to a great extent on our character.[43] He suggests that it is not merely the case that our moral deliberations will be seriously flawed if we do not perceive morally salient features,[44] deliberation itself will not occur if a person does not perceive a situation as morally problematic. Therefore, if de Sousa is correct, to define practical wisdom (*phronēsis*) in an unAristotelian manner, by neglecting considerations of excellences of character or moral virtue, is a mistake.

Epilogue

The view that business is primarily an economic institution was discussed in Chapters 2 and 4. The emphasis on material self-interest and the rejection of the emotions as a positive factor in business conduct have been connected traditionally with a concept called "rational economic man."[45] Edgar H. Schein suggests that four assumptions about human nature are entailed by this concept, but I shall consider the two that apply to feelings.

> Feelings are, by definition, 'irrational' and, therefore, must be prevented from interfering with a person's rational calculation of self-interest.... Organizations can and must be designed in such a way as to neutralize and control people's feelings and, therefore, their unpredictable traits.[46]

Feelings are excluded, then, from the realm of what is rational; they must be prevented at all costs from interfering with reason and with the rational functioning of organizations. I have shown that this dichotomy between feelings and rationality is incorrect. I should remind the reader that in Chapter 2, I gave examples of business theorists who complain about the heartlessness of business and discussed possible causes of this heartlessness. It would seem that businesspeople are unduly influenced by the view of feelings implied by the concept of rational economic man.

Given the prevalence of the notion of rational economic man among businesspeople and their general neglect of the importance of emotions, it might be helpful, in this epilogue, to supplement the previous discussion by considering the standard view of objective reasoning and showing that emotions are indispensable to it. If a person is asked why he thinks an opinion or belief is true or false, he is being asked to give reasons or evidence to defend his belief. Reasoning, then, involves justification, support, defense, proof, and the like. Since evidence can be either pro or con—that is, supporting or refuting evidence—objective reasoning is grounded in an attitude of looking at both sides of the evidence. On the other hand, the nonobjective reasoner has a prejudiced or biased attitude toward the evidence; he is concerned with supporting his pet beliefs.

Generally, objective reasoning entails open mindedness. A prejudiced or dogmatic person is unwilling to consider counter evidence. Thus, a rational person will not acquire habits which bias or warp her judgment. But it is not enough to be willing to consider counter evidence, one must be passionate about seeking it, as Socrates was. Open mindedness, as the prime requirement for rationality, is essentially to be open to criticism. Socrates recognizes that rational conversation progresses by falsification. One may find some evidence to defend a belief, but if there is legitimate counter evidence, the belief (logically speaking) must be modified. As Plato suggests, to show that one knows something, one must be able to run the gauntlet of legitimate objections. The rational person bends over backwards to defend opposing points of view. Open mindedness, then, helps the reasoner to develop the habit of searching for all the relevant evidence—to the degree to which this is possible and given such constraints as time and the importance of the issue at hand.[47]

It is difficult to believe that objective rationality is possible without support from requisite feelings or emotions. A lack of sympathy and empathy, for example, undermines open mindedness and encourages prejudice and dogmatism. This requires some elaboration.

Given the above analysis of the standard view of objective reasoning, a parallel can be shown to exist between it and moral sensibilities grounded in sympathy and empathy. John Dewey is particularly critical of exclusive dichotomies, and basing the source of moral conduct on either feeling or intellect is no exception. Dewey suggests the intimate connection between reason and feeling in a moral context. Sympathy (and one should include empathy) has been emphasized by moral sense theorists because it "carries thought out beyond the self and extends its scope ... [and] saves consideration of consequences from degenerating into mere calculation."[48] It helps "to put ourselves in the place of others, to see things from the standpoint of their purposes and values."[49] Sympathy is important, then, if we are to attain an objective, rational point of view.[50] "A union of benevolent impulse and intelligent reflection," says Dewey, "is the interest most likely to result in conduct that is good."[51]

Just as emotional openness to others supports the rational openness required by rational objectivity, so insensitivity, callousness or indifference towards qualities of persons or actions that are morally relevant causes one to neglect or distort morally relevant data, which a rational moral agent should consider. Moreover, even if reason does reach a correct conclusion on moral matters, such lack of feeling undermines any inclination to act in accordance with one's moral judgments.[52] One must conclude that if a businessperson believes in rational economic man, he or she is guided by a flawed notion of both a rational and a moral person. Certainly, the result of this position is an inadequate business ethic.

Rationality is rooted in habits which properly guide reflection and control biases. Practical rationality, however, is more than open mindedness; it also involves the ability to determine and achieve ends associated with human flourishing. It is often thought that when we are functioning rationally, we use practical reasoning to choose correct, efficient means for achieving desired ends. But if a desired end turns out to make us unhappy, the end is said to be irrational. Therefore, practical rationality implies both determining the correct means for achieving desired ends and aiming at those ends which promote what Aristotle calls human flourishing (*eudaimonia*).[53] The fact that we call ends rational or irrational suggests that a dichotomy which associates rationality exclusively with means and (irrational) desire and feeling with ends is wrong.[54] Section 2 of this chapter shows the essential incoherence of the dichotomy between practical rationality and emotion.

In this epilogue, I have attempted to supplement the discussion of emotion and practical rationality or the process of rational decision making with a consideration of how emotion is essential to rational objectivity. However, one can also argue for the importance of emotions in solving certain ethical dilemmas—and, therefore, in resolving certain ethical dilemmas in business.

Robert H. Frank believes that moral sentiments or emotions evolved to solve what he calls the "commitment problem."[55] This problem arises when material incentives at a specific time prompt people to behave contrary to their ultimate material interests. This dilemma is clearly relevant to business. However, such misleading material incentives can be countered by morally relevant emotions—emotions that relate to moral behavior, e.g., anger, contempt, disgust, shame, and guilt—and by opposing them, these emotions can aid us in achieving our material interests. The following are some of Frank's examples.[56]

1. Jones believes in rationally pursuing self-interest. If Smith steals his $200 briefcase, it will cost Jones $300 to convict him. Therefore, it is not in Jones material self-interest to sue Smith. Frank concludes, "Thus, if Smith knows Jones is a purely rational, self-interested person, he is free to steal the briefcase with impunity."[57] But suppose that Jones in not a pure "rationalist" and would be so outraged by such an injustice that he would sue Smith anyway. If Smith realizes this, he will not steal the briefcase. It is emotion, not rationality, that prevents the injustice.

2. Smith and Jones want to own a restaurant and can profitably form a partnership. Smith is a good cook but a poor manager. Jones is a poor cook but a good manager. Assuming each of them can cheat without detection, if one cheats and the other does not, he will do better. But if the victim also cheats, he will do better than if he does not cheat. However, they can both do much better if they do not cheat. Although a commitment not to cheat would yield the best result for both Smith and

Jones, narrow self-interest dictates cheating.[58] Emotions, however, can help to resolve this problem. If both potential restauranteurs are moved by shame or guilt and trust one another, the partnership will not exhibit the rationalist's dilemma.

3. Jones raises cattle on land that is adjacent to the property on which Smith grows wheat, and he is liable for whatever damage his steers do to Smith's wheat. Jones can fence in his land for $200 and thus protect himself from being sued. If he does not, the steers can eat $1,000 worth of Smith's wheat. Jones knows that if his steers eat the wheat, it will cost Smith $2,000 to sue him. If Jones believes that Smith is motivated by rational self-interest alone, Jones would dismiss Smith's threat to sue if Jones's cattle eat Smith's wheat. However, If Jones knows that Smith's rage and vengefulness will cause him to sue, he may well fence in his property.

4. Smith and Jones have the opportunity to engage in a joint venture which will net them $1,000. Jones has no pressing need for money but Smith does. Since Jones has the advantage, needing the money less, he can threaten that if he does not get, e.g., $800, he will not contract with Smith. It is in Smith's self-interest to agree. However, if Smith has a fierce sense of fairness, he may well decline Jones's offer; his outrage at Jones's unjust offer might offset the material incentive. Smith's stance might force a fairer split.

Emotions such as anger or outrage, therefore, can resolve some ethical dilemmas, which may result in an injustice to one of the involved parties, and shame and guilt can resolve some ethical dilemmas for mutual benefit. Emotions, then, are not only necessary for rational objectivity and practical rationality, they are also helpful in resolving certain ethical quandaries and achieving desired ends. Frank's examples of ethical dilemmas which are resolvable by emotions illustrate the danger of believing in rational economic man's view of feelings.

The following is worth mentioning. Emotions have often been accused of committing us to the short-term and, therefore, causing us to neglect our long-term advantages. Although this is sometimes true, certain emotions are necessary for achieving long-term advantages. Moral feelings or sentiments help us to pick potentially trustworthy partners. In general, moral sentiments are indispensable for gaining the benefits of cooperative endeavors. Virtuous people are attracted to one another and join forces for their mutual benefit. The more virtuous members of a society become, the more selfish people are rejected and left to their own fate.

Notes

1. Robert C. Solomon, *The Passions: Emotions and the Meaning of Life* (Indianapolis: Hackett Pub. Co., 1993), p. 11.

2. For the purpose of this chapter, the term "practical reason" or "practical reasoning" will be used to imply the ability to reason effectively in real life situations—situations in which decisions or choices are necessary.

3. In the last sixty years of Anglo-American metaethical theory, A. J. Ayer, Charles Stevenson, and R. M. Hare stand out as three of the most influential ethical theorists. Despite the fact that the former two philosophers maintain emotive theories of ethics, they exhibit a lack of understanding of the importance of emotions to practical reasoning.

    A basic concern of the logical positivists is to praise science and discredit metaphysics. Positivists such as A. J. Ayer think that this can be accomplished by offering a criterion of meaning such that scientific but not metaphysical sentences are literally meaningful; a sentence is literally meaningful, according to this criterion, if and only if it is capable of being true or false by being either analytic or empirically verifiable. Since they consider ethical judgments neither analytic nor empirically verifiable, such sentences are classed with metaphysical sentences as literal nonsense. According to Ayer, ethical judgments are emotive; they are expressions and excitants of feeling. Reason functions properly in the context of science; ethical judgments qua ethical—being emotive and therefore unverifiable—are not amenable to reason. Reasoning in ethics is effective only insofar as ethical disputes are based upon factual disagreements; factual disagreements can be rationally settled.

    Apart from the problem of formulating an adequate verifiability criterion, the positivists cannot show that their criterion of meaning is the way in which "meaning" is used, so they cannot cash in fairly on the usual connotations of "meaning." Indeed, they cannot even show that their criterion is one of the lexical senses of "meaning."

    Charles Stevenson's more sophisticated emotive theory of ethical judgments analyzes them into a descriptive and an emotive component; the purpose of the emotive element is to change or intensify attitudes. The emotive component is considered primary. According to Stevenson, it makes sense to ask for a justification of descriptions (or beliefs) but not of emotive sentences or components. Attitudes, for Stevenson, are fundamentally emotive and therefore, in his view, noncognitive.

But in ethical arguments, disagreement in attitude is fundamental, for such arguments are concerned with redirecting our opponent's attitudes. Since justificatory reasons are related to facts rather than emotions, he concludes that reasons in ethics are psychologically, not logically, related to ethical conclusions. Ethical disputes are resolvable only when disagreements in attitude are rooted in disagreements in belief. Reasoning is, again, allied with facts and radically separated from emotions and attitudes. As with Ayer, science and ethics exist in distinctly different spheres. This position is ironic, as we will see, for Antonio R. Damasio offers scientific evidence to defend the view that emotions are necessary conditions for practical reasoning.

Both Ayer and Stevenson, therefore, distinguish between emotions (and attitudes) as noncognitive and beliefs as cognitive (capable of being true or false). Reasoning in a logical sense pertains to (cognitive) beliefs but not to (noncognitive) emotions or attitudes. Even apart from the important counter evidence of Damasio and others considered in this chapter, this dichotomy is clearly indefensible. Attitudes can imply cognitive claims. For example, fear is related to a limited set of objects judged harmful and such a judgment is right or wrong depending upon whether the objects are harmful or not. The attitude of jealousy is related to certain specific objects and makes cognitive claims, i.e., A is claiming that X is enjoying favors from Y which A would like to have directed to himself.

Both Ayer and Stevenson recognize the fact that ethical judgments purport to guide action; they are practical. Emotions certainly fill the bill. R. M. Hare, however, believing that reasoned ethical argument is possible, wants to distinguish between causes and reasons—a distinction he believes Stevenson does not clearly make. Recognizing that he too must explain the action-guiding nature of ethical judgments, he uses prescriptivity as the essential element in ethical judgments. For example, the primary meaning of "good," he suggests, is commendation (the prescriptive element); the secondary meaning is the criterion for its application (the descriptive meaning). Since the former is not logically tied to the latter—this would violate the "no ought from is" rule—one is not logically obligated to commend on the basis of any specific criterion or set of descriptions. To commend some ethical criterion is to make a decision to accept it.

Although Hare does present a carefully formulated theory of ethical argument, which depends upon what one can consistently universalize, G. J. Warnock notes a difficulty in his theory. Both Stevenson and Hare make it possible to *decide* what the evidence is [*Contemporary Moral Philosophy* (London: MacMillan, 1967), p. 47]. Such a position is inconsistent with the accepted view of objective reasoning. One should note that, according to Hare, rationality in ethics is possible because the descriptive element in moral judgments is universalizable. The prescriptive element in moral judgments, which is primary, is nonrational. Therefore, Ayer, Stevenson, and Hare all agree that the primary element in ethical judgments is nonrational. How different are the views of Stevenson and Hare? Although it may be argued that Hare's view of ethical reasoning is more sophisticated than Stevenson's, and he believes that the "emotivity" of moral judgments is an unreliable symptom of the evaluative use of words, their positions on ethical judgments would be similar if prescriptivity entails emotions. Warnock argues plausibly that "in the case of prescriptive discourse, actions confirm or refute words" (Warnock, p. 37). This is the case because prescriptions entail imperatives. If in prescriptive, and therefore moral, discourse, there is this close connection between words, e.g., expressing moral beliefs, and actions, could this connection even exist without emotions? If, as Damasio shows, emotions or feelings are at least a necessary condition for translating moral beliefs into actions, Hare's putative advance over emotive theories is illusory.

4. I have argued for an Aristotelian virtue ethics approach to business ethics in Chapter 3. The reader should keep this discussion of Aristotle in mind while reading this chapter.

5. Antonio R. Damasio, *Descartes' Error* (New York: G. P. Putnam's Sons, 1994). The case is well known and appears, for example, in many introductory psychology texts. Damasio is a professor of neurology who, with his wife Hanna, founded a leading facility for the study of neurological disorders of mind and behavior.

6. Damasio, p. 8.

7. Damasio, p. 11. In an earlier passage, referring to Gage's post-accident personality, Damasio says, "He was now 'fitful, irreverent, indulging at times in the grossest profanity which was not previously his custom, manifesting but little deference for his fellows, impatient of restraint or advice when it conflicts with his desires, at times pertinaciously obstinate, yet capricious and vacillating, devising many plans of future operations, which are no sooner arranged than they are abandoned'" (Damasio, p. 8).

8. The research of his wife, Hanna Damasio, and her colleagues shows that damage to Gage's ventromedial prefrontal region explains his impaired ability to make practical decisions.

9. Thus, any attempt to use the rational/irrational distinction to differentiate cognition and emotion is doomed to failure. Also see Joseph LeDoux, *The Emotional Brain: The Mysterious Underpinnings of Emotional Life* (New York: Simon and Schuster, 1996), pp. 36–37.

10. Damasio, p. viii.

11. Damasio, p. 35.

12. Damasio, p. 45.

13. This issue has a bearing on my criticism of teleological and/or deontological approaches to business ethics.

14. Damasio, pp. 48–49.

15. Damasio, p. 46. Damasio's colleague, Paul Eslinger, devised a series of controlled laboratory tests to determine both a person's ability to conceive of alternative solutions to hypothetical social problems and his or her awareness of consequences. In the former test, Elliot performed as well as the control group, and in the latter, his performance was superior. Moreover, Elliot performed "impeccably" on tasks for determining efficacious means for achieving a social goal.

16. Damasio says, "To date we have studied twelve patients with prefrontal damage of the type seen in Elliot, and in none have we failed to encounter a combination of decision-making defect and flat emotion and feeling" (Damasio, pp. 53–54). He also considers animal studies to support his thesis. In addition, it should be noted that Damasio shows that this combination of impairments can be produced by damage to other parts of the brain, e.g., damage to the right cerebral hemisphere and to the limbic system.

17. Aristotle maintains this view in the *Nicomachean Ethics*. Damasio believes that to decide well, here, is intimately related to selecting responses that are advantageous to a person's survival and to the quality of that survival, directly or indirectly. Damasio says, "Whenever I call a decision advantageous, I refer to basic personal and social outcomes such as survival of the individual and its kin, the securing of shelter, the maintenance of physical and mental health, employment and financial solvency, and good standing in the social group. Gage's and Elliot's new mind no longer permitted them to obtain any of these advantages" (Damasio, p. 170).

18. I think that Plato is a more complicated case than Damasio suggests. Nonetheless, his belief that Aristotle is no Cartesian is correct. Damasio says, "How annoyed Aristotle would have been with Descartes [the radical separation of mind and body], had he known" (Damasio, p. 251).

19. Damasio, p. 171.

20. Damasio, p. 171.

21. Damasio, p. 172.

22. Damasio also suggests that sociopaths or psychopaths, who are unfeeling and uncaring, "are the very picture of the cool head we were told to keep in order to do the right thing" (Damasio, p. 178).

23. Damasio says, "Because the feeling is about the body, I give the phenomenon the technical term *somatic* state ('soma' is Greek for body); and because it 'marks' an image, I called it a *marker*" (Damasio, p. 173).

   Damasio believes that all ideas are images. "Having a mind," says Damasio, "means that an organism forms neural representations which can become images, be manipulated in a process called thought, and eventually influence behavior by helping to predict the future, plan accordingly, and choose the next action" (Damasio, p. 90). On the basis of these images, we can interpret sensory signals so that we may organize them as concepts and categorize them. We can, then, develop strategies for reasoning and decision making and select motor responses from available options (Damasio, p. 93).

In Damasio's Humean mind, then, "the factual knowledge required for reasoning and decision-making comes to mind in the form of images" (Damasio, p. 96); these images can be formed from sense perceptions or from what is conjured up in remembering the past or thinking about the future. Metaphysically speaking, all we can know are the psychic constructions of a world based upon the constitution of our organism.

24.   Damasio, p. 174. As one might suspect, Damasio maintains that "the critical neural system for the acquisition of somatic-marker signaling is in the prefrontal cortices ..." (Damasio, p. 180).

25.   Damasio distinguishes between primary and secondary emotions. Primary emotions are automatic responses which, therefore, do not necessitate the intervention of consciousness or feeling; feeling, he suggests, involves the consciousness of emotion. (However, Damasio also posits a type of nonemotional feeling he calls "background feelings.") Secondary emotions do involve consciousness and are mediated, therefore, by mental images. It is these emotions, rather than primary emotions, that patients with prefrontal damage, e.g., Gage and Elliot, cannot generate; that is, they cannot produce emotions which, in their normal condition, they exhibited to certain mental images conjured up by certain situations and stimuli. In consequence, they cannot have the related feelings.

26.   Not only is reason alone incapable of limiting the possible choices to a manageable number, by itself, it cannot determine when to start or stop cost/benefit analyses.

27.   Damasio, p. 173. The following is a clear illustration of the awareness of this point as it pertains to business. At the very beginning of the Forward to Tom Peter's, *The Circle of Innovation* (N.Y.: Alfred A. Knopf, 1997), Dean Le Baron says, "Business— successful business—is more visceral than cerebral.... Tom Peters is more visceral than cerebral. He feels business in his gut.... What distinguishes Tom is this: passion and passionate energy. He moves when he sees opportunity. He hurts when he sees mediocrity. He exalts when he sees innovation" (p. viii).

28.   One may note that Ronald de Sousa gives a very positive review of *Descartes' Error* [in Volume 6 (2) of *The Semiotic Review of Books*].

29.   Ronald de Sousa, *The Rationality of Emotions* (Cambridge: The MIT Press, 1987), p. 190.

30.   de Sousa, *The Rationality of Emotions*, p. 191.

31. "Emotions are species of determinate patterns of salience among objects of attention, lines of inquiry, and inferential strategies" (de Sousa, *The Rationality of Emotions*, p. 196).

    Israel Scheffler agrees with Damasio and de Sousa. Emotions, he maintains, serve "a *selective* function, facilitating choice among these [imaginative] patterns, defining their salient features, focusing attention accordingly" [*In Praise of the Cognitive Emotions and Other Essays in the Philosophy of Education* (New York: Routledge, 1991), p. 8].

32. Like de Sousa, Dennett praises *Descartes' Error*. See Dennett's review of *Descartes' Error* in the *Times Literary Supplement*, August 25, 1995, pp. 3–4.

33. de Sousa, *The Rationality of Emotions*, pp. 193–194.

34. de Sousa, *The Rationality of Emotions*, p. 194.

35. de Sousa, *The Rationality of Emotions*, p. xv. Emotion compensates for reason's inefficiency by limiting "the range of information that the organism will take into account, the inferences actually drawn from a potential infinity, and the set of live options among which it will choose" (de Sousa, *The Rationality of Emotions*, p. 195).

36. Damasio, pp. 245–246.

37. Scheffler, p. 4.

38. Scheffler, p. 5.

39. Damasio suggests that some cultures are "sick" and therefore can pervert moral reasoning.

40. Damasio suggests that sometimes when we act in character we are not conscious of the mechanism involved in choice. In Damasio's language, there is a covert mechanism of positive and negative reactions that causes us to function intuitively rather than by rational analysis.

41. de Sousa, *The Rationality of Emotions*, p. 305.

42. de Sousa, *The Rationality of Emotions*, p. 305.

43. Sometimes our lack of perception may not be due to deficiencies in character. We may, at a specific time, be self-absorbed or we may be in a crowded situation and we tune out in crowds or we may not have accurate information about a person and thus misperceive morally relevant factors; one may enumerate a number of other reasons. For a good treatment of this issue, see Lawrence A. Blum, *Moral*

Perception and Particularity (Cambridge: Cambridge University Press, 1994).

44. I do not think that there is a faculty of moral perception. The notion of character is complex so that one may be more sensitive to some morally relevant features of a situation than to others. The more highly developed a person's moral character, the less particularized will be his or her moral sensitivities and therefore perceptions.

45. Clarence C. Walton says, "The modern corporation is in many respects the twentieth-century equivalent of Adam Smith's eighteenth-century *homo oeconomicus*" [*Ethos and the Executive: Values in Managerial Decision Making* (Englewood Cliffs, New Jersey: Prentice-Hall, Inc., 1969), p. 72]. Classical free enterprise theory assumes, among other things, that each person is primarily motivated by economic self-interest, and given economic freedom, this pursuit of narrow self-interest best ensures economic progress. This notion of economic man is conceptually related to the idea of rational economic man. An economic man will act rationally in that he will know when an option(s) serves his best interests and will act upon it.

46. Edgar H. Schein, *Organizational Psychology*, 3rd ed. (Englewood Cliffs, New Jersey: Prentice-Hall, 1980), p. 53.

47. Open mindedness is also related to being logical, that is, drawing out implications from relevant evidence and detecting errors in inferences.

48. John Dewey, *Theory of the Moral Life* (New York: Holt, Rinehart and Winston, 1960), pp. 129–130.

49. Dewey, p. 130.

50. However, unregulated by reflection, sympathy degenerates into sentimentality. The sentimental person is a simplistic parody of the moral person.

   We may note in passing that Plato and Aristotle believe that emotions play an important part in objective reasoning. In this chapter, I stress the importance of Aristotelian ethics for business ethics. However, in this context, I could have also argued for the importance of Platonic ethics. In the *Republic* (402a), Plato suggests that there is a kinship between his proposed character education and rationality. For Plato, a rational person's thinking exhibits due measure or proportion; a rational mind is a properly balanced mind. Platonic character education creates a prereflective affinity for rationality by nurturing a distaste for excessive appetites and emotions. Similarly, Aristotle's famous doctrine of the mean (which is also Platonic) is directed against excessive passions. More positively, proper character development disciplines emotions and appetites; it creates a correct emotional balance or proportion. Thus, for Plato, fine character reflects the due measure or proportion exhibited by objective reason; fine character provides a necessary condition for a balanced reason.

51. Dewey, p. 163. In general, to say that morality is either a matter of feeling (or emotion) or reason is as much a reductionist mistake as to argue that businesspeople are nothing but economic animals.

52. See, for example, Dewey, p. 128.

53. Plato and Aristotle (I think correctly) believe that emotions in general, and not just empathy and sympathy, must be habituated so that human actions are guided towards the correct target, human flourishing.

54. Any attempt to radically separate knowledge and desire or feeling fails. If the desire for X is rational, then X is both attainable and will bring some satisfaction. Thus, to desire X when it is unattainable and/or unsatisfying is irrational. Desire, then, contains both cognitive and affective or feeling elements; it moves us only in conjunction with knowledge.

55. Robert H. Frank, *Passions within Reason: Strategic Role of Emotions* (New York: W. W. Norton and Co., 1988), see, for example, P. 47.

56. See Frank, pp. x, 47–49, 53–54.

57. Frank, p. x.

58. This is a clear example of the prisoner's dilemma. I mention this problem because the prisoner's dilemma is the type of game that has influenced many business thinkers. [See, for example, Robert C. Solomon, *Ethics and Excellence:Cooperation and Integrity in Business* (New York: Oxford University Press, 1993), p. 57.]

    The prisoner's dilemma posits two prisoners who are self-interested. If neither gives evidence against the other, each can only be convicted on a lesser charge. If one confesses and the second does not, the first will receive a greatly reduced term while the second will get a maximum sentence. If both confess, both receive a moderate sentence (but more than if both remained silent). Although cooperation would yield the best result (the least amount of prison time for both), each reasons that he is better off if he confesses rather than remains silent because if one confesses and the other doesn't, the one who doesn't confess is in for the maximum sentence. Thus, the prisoner's dilemma purports to show that although cooperation yields the optimum result, acting in accordance with one's own (rational) self-interest results in a lack of cooperation. This putative conclusion of the prisoner's dilemma, however, is not correct.

    It was discovered that when the prisoner's dilemma is played as a computer game more than once, cooperation, not defection of both partners was the result. Moreover, more sophisticated computer versions of this game lead to the same result. In our example, it is interesting to note that it is emotions that help to produce the truly rational (optimum) result—cooperation.

Index

Studies in Theoretical and Applied Ethics

Sherwin Klein, General Editor

This series invites book manuscripts and proposals in English on either theoretical or applied ethics. Books submitted on traditional moral philosophers or on one or more ethical problems they have considered are welcome. However, authors should demonstrate strong connections between historical and contemporary philosophical concerns in ethics. Preference will be given to works which deal with perennial philosophical issues in ethics in an original, clear, and scholarly manner rather than manuscripts which have historical significance alone. Books which approach applied ethics, e.g., business and biomedical ethics, from a philosophical perspective are also welcome. Manuscripts should display expertise in both philosophy and the areas illuminated by the philosophical insights.

Please send manuscripts and proposals with author's vitae to

Sherwin Klein
Edward Williams College
Fairleigh Dickinson University
150 Kotte Place
Hackensack, NJ 07601

To order other books in this series, please contact our Customer Service Department:

(800) 770-LANG (within the U.S.)
(212) 647-7706 (outside the U.S.)
(212) 647-7707 FAX

Or browse online by series:

www.peterlangusa.com